W9-BZW-427

# Keeping School

# Keeping School

## LETTERS TO FAMILIES FROM PRINCIPALS OF TWO SMALL SCHOOLS

*Deborah Meier*
*Theodore R. Sizer*
*Nancy Faust Sizer*

BEACON PRESS | *Boston*

Beacon Press
25 Beacon Street
Boston, Massachusetts
02108-2892
www.beacon.org

Beacon Press books are published under the auspices of the Unitarian Universalist Association of Congregations.



07 06 05 04    8 7 6 5 4 3 2 1

This book is printed on acid-free paper that meets the uncoated paper ANSI/NISO specifications for permanence as revised in 1992.

Composition by Wilsted & Taylor Publishing Services

Library of Congress Cataloging-in-Publication Data

Meier, Deborah.
Keeping school : letters to families from principals of two small schools / Deborah Meier, Nancy Faust Sizer, Theodore R. Sizer.
p. cm.
ISBN 0-8070-3264-6
(cloth : alk. paper)
1. Small schools—United States. 2. Teaching—United States. 3. School management and organization—United States. I. Sizer, Nancy Faust. II. Sizer, Theodore R. III. Title.

LB3012.5.M45 2004
371.102—dc22    2004000713

# Contents

# Introduction

*Theodore R. Sizer*

Schools are wonderfully complicated places.

Even an orderly appearance that a visitor might observe masks the inevitable muddle arising from the incessant banging of dozens of egos, small and large, in one of our culture's most densely packed workplaces.

*You took my book. No I didn't. I don't get this. Try it again. I still don't get this, and everybody else has. I am stupid. No, you are not stupid. I got it! I got it!*

*I will not do that. I was not yelling. He did it. Be cool, man. My teacher, he's cool. I want to be like her when I grow up. Stay away. Don't bother me. Let me read. Can I join?*

*This is boring, boring, boring. This is neat, let's try it again.*

*I love taking care of Mr. Dan's snakes and rats in his class-*

*room. Yuck, you can see the bulge of the rat in the snake! I am pumped to play Cleopatra. I got the part. Janey didn't. Ha ha!*

*Don't push me. I didn't. You did. No, I didn't.*

*No one asked me what I thought. No one explained that to me. No, I will not try to do it again. I can hardly wait for the game. I am going to be terrific. I dread the test. I dread that class that never seems to settle down. No one respects me. I am not stupid. Listen to me! I got it! I got it!*

*My kids don't get it. I need more time. That class took off in ways that I never dreamed. Now what to do with those kids? What's up with Gloria? Why is she suddenly so sullen?*

*That teacher won't tell me anything about Rose. I'm her mother; doesn't she understand that!*

*I couldn't believe that was my son's work; he's a real young man now.*

In schools there are people of all ages, all on show, trying to make sense of themselves and their compatriots.

Constructive quiet is a school's stereotypic norm, the silences invaded only by the measured words of a teacher's lecture or the subdued but constructive babbling of children; but even within this mock serenity, the medley of individualities intrudes. John reacts differently than does Carlos. Susan isn't her buoyant self today. The neatly planned lesson collapses. The place may be quiet but inside the minds of many children will be a cacophony. And schools are about influencing those minds.

Capturing the best of this constructive individuality—an American ideal—while maintaining the purposeful calm that is necessary for each child's and each teacher's concentration is no easy task, and it takes somewhat different form day to day, even minute to minute. Schools are not machines that can be exquisitely tuned in advance and then allowed to run in a dependably consistent way. Schools are places constantly in motion, with the unexpected being expected.

Many, including the three of us, call the handling of this wonderfully complicated explosion of individualities the keeping of school. We like that gerund better than other, familiar characterizations.

A more commonly used verb is "run." I run my school (or my classroom). I-the-Principal am its Manager. Neat and convenient though this characterization can be, it is misleading. No higher authority can wholly command or tune or oil up or operate—whatever might be synonymous with run—a place both so physically sprawled and full of all those big and little people, most of them at best crudely disciplined that fill a school. And school people cannot just walk away from this cacophony, pushing it aside, smothering those egos. Our job as teachers and principals is to understand and then to harness these budding egos, whatever crop of them might appear in our classrooms. "Run" implies more order than we believe is either necessary or proper.

Another verb is "provide." Districts provide schools. But that word is too passive, too static for our taste. Having a school is more than just furnishing a place and staff. Carefully though we may prepare, schools are hostages to even small currents of change: a winning (or losing) soccer season, the arrival of several recent immigrants to this country, none of whom speaks English and all of whom are terribly frightened; the serious illness of a student; a national catastrophe; a fight in the cafeteria. No school can just ignore these matters, even if it tries to do so. Everyone in a school is affected by them, whatever the precise "schedule" might require. The school changes, usually in small ways, sometimes in large ones.

And so we settle on keeping—Keeping School—as the word "keep" has a wonderful range of germane shadings. It means taking in (in the sense of watching out for). It denotes management (as in keeping house) and persistence (as in keeping at something). It implies the storing of things, sometimes to protect them (as the keep in a castle). It implies holding fast (keeping faith). It describes the provision of sustenance—in a school's case, intellectual and moral sustenance, the gathering of adults, teachers mostly, around the task of lifting up the children.

We surely did not invent its use for education. That goes back several centuries, at least to William Shakespeare who employed it in a similar (albeit comic) context in *Twelfth Night* (Act III, Scene ii, 81). Its richness suggests active and humane qualities that we admire much more than are implied in words such as run and provide. And we believe that language profoundly shapes schools: Using the word "keep" says what we want said about our collective craft. Principals and teachers manage—indeed, shepherd—schools, usually with carefully outlined routines and schedules but (at our best) softened with the flexibility required to respond to unexpected troubles, opportunities, or the angularities that are found among children and adults. The best of us persist at this complex work, faithful to our charge but flexible within it. We watch and listen and adapt to an immediate hour's potentialities and distractions, to the children, to their families, to our expectations, and to the expectations of the community and of the state.

We principals and teachers know, however, that our ministrations are but a slice of a student's life, and rarely a large slice. We are minority partners in the education of the young. We share each student with her parents and guardians; and as that child grows into adolescence, we increasingly share her with the media, with the peer group, with jobs, and with the street. Even if the child is with us every school day for six hours, in the course of a year we directly affect barely a fourth of her waking hours. It follows, then, that if our students are to learn well we must make as many alliances as possible with the adults who shape these other venues. None of these adults is more important than those found in the student's home. We believe that if school and family are respectful allies, all will benefit, and especially the child. To be allies, we have to communicate.

The three of us have all been teachers and principals. In that latter role especially we tried hard to make and sustain close contact with students' families. A key vehicle that Deborah has long used and that Nancy and I copied from her and others was a weekly letter home to parents, the purpose of which was to explain what was happening at school and why. We hoped that our writing might generate parental reactions that could lead to contacts between us on matters that we all believed were important to the school.

These brief letters reflected immediate issues, often very humble ones, sometimes grander ones, of politics and policy. As you will see, few could have been written in a prior summer and issued on the basis of a long-range schedule. Of necessity they are time- and situation-bound. They emerged from the immediate complexities of two public schools, an urban elementary school (for Deborah), an exurban public secondary school (for Nancy and me), both in Massachusetts.

Our hope in this book is to display a selection of these letters exactly as they were written in the hope that they will communicate a sense of what it is to "keep school." We trust that the sum of these letters, and the essays and commentary we have added to them, will manifest some important values that the three of us share for our students. We also hope that many families, teachers, and principals will find them persuasive, pertinent, and provocative.

What brought the three of us together over two decades ago were convictions about schooling, learning, and children. In 1984 Deborah was the principal of a New York City elementary school and the architect of a network of like-minded schools, all progressive in design and summarized by the word "collaborative." At a celebration on the occasion of the tenth birthday of this gathering of New York schools, I encouraged Deborah to follow through on her dream of creating a public secondary school in East Harlem to be designed, albeit for older children, around the same ideas that had informed her and her colleagues' elementary schools.

Deborah had already started on that challenge. Supported by friends and two risk-taking superintendents, Anthony Alvarado and Carlos Medina, she, again with sturdy colleagues, designed and launched Central Park East Secondary School, a place that over the next two decades was to gather international attention. CPESS (an acronym pronounced "spess") was one of the first and most influential members of the Coalition of Essential Schools, a national gathering of middle and high schools committed to a common set of principles that had been distilled from research carried out by me and many colleagues over the preceding years. Behind these principles rested the belief that there was not, nor could there ever be, a single One Good Secondary School Model. The most persuasive strong high schools, we had concluded, while having some critical ideas in common, reflected the geniuses of their own settings, each school resonating the best (or worst) of its particular community of children, teachers, and families. No two such good (or bad) schools were quite alike, any more than any two wonderful (or dysfunctional) families are ever quite alike.

The common principles were uncontroversial in substance but usually difficult to put into practice. Focus was to be on the intellect, guiding the students into the habit of using their minds well in all aspects of their lives. To

# MISSION HILL SCHOOL NEWS

Week of January 28, 2002 — Vol. 5, No. 20

## REMINDERS

- **Friday, February 1:** Auditions for 2002 Alvin Ailey Summer Camp for 5th, 6th and 7th graders after morning assembly
- **Wednesday, February 6:** Governance Board meeting and vote on co-principal process, open to whole school community, 5:30–6:00 p.m.
- **Thursday, February 7:** "How our kids learn math" with Hollee Freeman of Young Achievers, sponsored by Parent Council, 6–8 p.m. in school library.
- **Tuesday, February 12:** West House family night, 5:45 p.m.
- **February 16 through 24:** Winter school vacation.
- **Tuesday, February 26:** East House family night, 5:45 p.m.
- **Week of March 4:** Family conferences.
- **Week of March 18:** 4th and 5th grades to Farm School.

**Mission Hill T-Shirts**
**Black w/ silver letters**
**Blue w/ silver letters**
**Kid sizes 10/12, 14/16**
**Adult sizes S to XL**
**$10 each**

***See Maria in the Office***

LETTER FROM MISSION HILL

## Four Arguments Against the Tests

Dear Families, Students, Staff, and Friends,

Two weeks ago, I wrote that the current test mania in the U.S. is doing more and more harm. I want to be very clear about the reasons I feel so strongly about standardized testing.

1. Standardized tests are being used improperly, in ways that were never intended. They were designed to measure "I.Q." or "aptitude"—something fixed, to be measured once or twice in a lifetime. That idea itself is suspect. But as James Popham, a leading test expert, says, mere cosmetic changes like calling them "achievement" tests don't change what they're able to do. Robert Linn, another leader in testing, reminds us that, above all, they were never designed to be "taught to."

2. The measurement error is enormous. The same test given to the same student on a different day can yield a wildly different score. Averaged over a large population, these errors tend to balance each other out. But the tests are invalid at the individual score level.

3. The multiple-choice, right/wrong format can't capture achievement. Neither can mini-essays scored by people who must read them in a minute or less. These features of standardized tests make them fast and cheap to administer and score, but they compound their inaccuracy.

4. Standardized tests exclude most of what, in the real world (including college), defines being well-educated.

It's as if we decided that the written portion of the driver's test was all that mattered, and we spent all our energy in driver's ed raising kids' scores on that part. Then, to make sure no one thought we were going soft, we made the questions really hard (how does fuel injection affect performance of catalytic converters?) and added open-ended writing tasks (describe what to do when your left rear tire blows out while driving at 55 miles per hour). Then, just to show you were raising standards, you counted spelling and punctuation. Fine. But such a test wouldn't actually distinguish a good from a bad driver.

Ditto for these tests. They miss everything that matters: reading with a critical mind, not getting fooled by nonsense, and knowing how to persuade, work well with others, take leadership, stick to a task, meet deadlines, be reliable in a crunch, or take initiative.

*What if we decided that the written part of the driver's test was all that mattered?*

The tests are good for one thing: ranking people (and schools, and districts). And they have always done a good job of making sure the winners in the rest of life's stakes stay ahead and the losers stay behind. That's not by accident. (More on that later.)

So Mission Hill is sticking with tests of actual performance—the things that really count. We'll teach kids some of the tricks of testing, partly because they're interesting and partly because if kids take tests they should know a bit about how they work. —*Deborah Meier*

*The Mission Hill School is a pilot school of the Boston Public Schools*

Deborah Meier, Principal
Brian Straughter, Assistant Principal
Maria Gaines-Harris, Office Manager
Thomas Payzant, Superintendent
67 Alleghany Street
Roxbury, MA 02120
Main Office: 617-635-6384

accomplish this, the goals of what came to be known as an Essential school had to apply to every student and had to be simple, clear, and focused. What they had to be focused on—primarily and in combination—was the classic core of traditional secondary schooling—language, history, mathematics, sciences, the arts, ideally all inte-

P.O. Box 2129
Devens, MA 01432
(978) 772-3293
(978) 772-3295 fax
www.parker.org

Theodore R. Sizer, *principal*
Nancy Faust Sizer, *co-principal*



**Friday Announcements** **Date: January 8, 1999**

Dear Families,

I couldn't get over the change in one of my grandchildren during the vacation. He ate his dinner with nary a complaint, then weasled as much dessert out of me as he could manage, and followed it up with a bowl of cereal! When he asked for another bowl, I could only stare at him. "Growth spurt," he airily explained.

His sister, who is one whole minute older, is on a different kind of growth spurt these days. It concerns the bravery with which she tackles the ski slopes. The two of them also trade off growth spurts in reading and math, in no discernible order and — sometimes — depending on their teachers. They don't expect to develop at the same rate in everything. But they started the year in fourth grade, and they will stay in fourth grade until June.

At Parker, we like to say, smugly, we do better. Each student is invited to progress at his own rate. If her work is solid and thorough, her portfolio and her habits of learning at an appropriate level, she may petition to gateway into a new division in the middle of the year. On that basis, more than one hundred students will change one, two or even three classes this month. This is a policy of the school which is taken for granted by students and has been strongly endorsed by parents in surveys and forums over the years.

There is another aspect of schoolkeeping, however, which is somewhat compromised by the policy of midyear gateways. It is subtler, harder to explain, but also very important. The classes which start off together in the beginning of the year are small communities. As they gel, and the students and their teachers begin to trust each other, learning increases. The interests, talents and behaviors of each person become part of a rich blend which, usually, grows more smooth and functional as the class marches together through a set of experiences and challenges. This learning is slower and less dramatic, but it, too, is a vital part of our craft.

Where are the patterns? Any school with at least two good ideas in it will sometimes find them to be at odds with each other. In this case, we have decided to honor individual progress over stability and community-building in our classes. We recognize, however, that some non-gatewayers will be affected by the alterations which we must make to their schedules. We are working to minimize the disruption in every way we can. We will also need your help as counselors, so that your children will be able not only to adjust to the changes in their classes but also to understand the ways in which both growth and collaboration fit into the context of our educational philosophy.

Nancy

grated. To the fullest possible extent, the teaching was to be personalized, each child learning and moving in his or her most effective way and progressing at his or her best speed, no faster (endangering superficiality) or slower (provoking boredom) than wise. Because every child was assumed (accurately) to have "special needs," each one had a personal learning plan. Promotion for each child depended upon demonstration of mastery of the skills articulated in the plan rather than simply being a year older. That demonstration of intellectual habits required that the student had fully to engage at the task of his learning.

We used the phrase "student as worker, teacher as coach." The youngsters had to engage, and we teachers had to "tell" less often and "coach" more often. This required us teachers to ascertain precisely what a standard was in an area—that is, what was acceptable written prose, say, for an early teenager—and we had to invent devices to ascertain when that standard was met; it could not be satisfied by a single performance but required the steady *habit* of such performances. We knew that we had to work collaboratively; no one of us had all the answers about each child.

Deborah's CPESS explicitly defined its version of these intellectual habits and imbued its message into all aspects of the school:

Concern for Evidence (How do you know that?)
Viewpoint (Who said it and why?)
Cause and effect (What led to it? What else happened?)
Hypothesizing (What if? Supposing what?)
So what? (Who cares? Do we care? Do I care? Why?)

Such imperatives profoundly change the way one perceives school, from a place that "delivers content and skills" to a place that "engenders the habits of the informed use of knowledge." The shift in emphasis is not just rhetorical; it has substantial implications for practice.

It also affects how school proceeds. If the children are to be known well, each teacher must have no more of them than he or she can "know well"—a number that I originally pegged for secondary schools at no more than eighty but today believe is no more than fifty—and that remain with that teacher for a substantial period of time. Specific mechanisms make this possible in many different settings: block scheduling; multiple grade levels in a classroom in the lower grades; teachers teaching more than one subject, like math and science, together. There must be time for my colleagues and me to discuss how each child is progressing and for a school culture that secures the collegiality necessary for frank, principled, and constructive dialogue. In practice, then, this requires a simply designed school, one not ruled by minutes and bells but flexibly driven by the demands of learning a few essentially important matters enduringly well. It requires graduation to be on the basis of a public Exhibition, the expression by a student that she not only has "covered" important areas of knowledge but can deploy them accurately even when confronted by unfamiliar questions from strangers. Such a skill is, of course, the "real world" for which we are preparing our students. You will see these topics discussed in the letters and essays that follow.

To accomplish this, the scale of the school (or autonomous unit within a big school building) had to be small. Principals and teachers had to be generalists as well as specialists. The subtlest requirements of the Coalition's principles were the most difficult: "The tone of the school should explicitly and self-consciously stress values of unanxious expectation ('I won't threaten you, but I expect much of you'), of trust (until abused), and of decency (the values of fairness, generosity, and tolerance)."

While Deborah was launching CPESS and I was superintending and studying the spread of Essential school ideas while teaching at Brown University, Nancy was well into her second decade of high-school teaching at the Wheeler School in Providence. She had started her career at a city public school in Cambridge (then called Cambridge High and Latin School), thence to a small public high school, the Bromfield School, in Harvard, Massachusetts, and thence to Phillips Academy, where I was for nine years headmaster and history teacher. Each of these schools was, more or less, in its own way, provocative and effective. In all, the twenty-five years of practice in varied settings deeply attuned Nancy to what made sense, what didn't, and what might explain the difference. In 1996, Nancy and I retired from our work in Providence and moved back to the small town in central Massachusetts, which had always been our emotional home. Old friends of ours who were neighbors—two of whom were experienced with Essential schools work—and who had children at the threshold of middle school were eager to start a public charter school as newly authorized under the Massachusetts Education Reform Act of 1993. They asked Nancy and me to join them, giving our group what Deborah had experienced in New York: a chance to design from scratch a "grade 7–12" secondary school shaped by Essential school principles. This nascent board of trustees won a charter and in 1994 opened the doors of the Francis W. Parker Charter Essential School. The school was housed in a windowless building ("2602") on what had since 1917 been called Fort Devens; the base had recently been abandoned by the United States Army. Like most utterly new and underfinanced ventures, the school got off to a bumpy start. To lend our hands at steadying it, Nancy and I, already trustees, agreed to serve for as acting co-principals for the 1998–99 academic year, during which time the state inspectors would recommend on the school's continuation or closure.

In 1996, on the invitation of Thomas Payzant, Boston Public Schools superintendent, Deborah was lured away from New York to start a new, small elementary school. The Coalition of Essential Schools had by that time created a set of principles appropriate to elementary education, close kin to the earlier list. Deborah's new school was to be an Essential school as well as a "Pilot" school (as designated within the city's contract with the Boston Teachers Union) and thus prepared to break, where necessary, new ground. Mission Hill School opened its doors in September, 1997.

Deborah's letters that follow draw on her several years at Mission Hill. Nancy's and mine draw only from the 1998–99 academic year when we served as Parker acting co-principals. As is apparent, these two small public schools, however different in venue and in student ages served, are both Essential schools and thereby share a substantial and fundamental core of ideas and commitments.

Rereading these letters a few years later, we are drawn

to their specificity and to how much we cared when we wrote them. They illustrate the wide variety of issues that come up in new idea-driven, community-influenced schools. The letters concern democracy and behavior, culture and individualism, assessment and progress, daily practice and state policy. They are expressions of the delight we took and take in being in these child-filled places, of our pride in the atmosphere of caring that each school has managed to create, and of our determination to overcome the obstacles that are still in our way. They reflect the commitment to democracy that guides both of our schools as places of collective responsibility (from the eldest to the youngest) and shared decision making (teachers, students, parents, concerned neighbors), places that both listened and heard, that explained what and why they believed and did, that recognized and respected difference, and that encouraged civil discussion of matters, however sometimes painful, that affected us all.

Each week as we wrote these letters we were constantly reminded of the important collaboration that needs to exist among the teachers and parents who are trying to help children to achieve honorable adulthood. Further, these letters bear witness to the idea of school as a cultural and intellectual community that can serve as a sturdy, exemplary foundation for children—and, along the way, for us, their parents, and their teachers.

It is practice that engenders the deepest form of philosophy, or so we (and John Dewey, among others) have long argued. In publishing these letters, we want to pursue the idea of keeping school, reflecting again upon these richly complicated places.

We ask ourselves: What areas of our school's mission need to be tackled and articulated, again and again? How do we explain our school's mores to new parents as well as those who have been involved with the school for years? When should confusion—ours, particularly—be admitted? When does one have to be grandmotherly or grandfatherly, experienced, an expert, telling It how we believe It is? What information is necessary for parents to have? What might unduly worry or inappropriately embarrass them? How do the schools' leaders, who insist that each person in the community deserves respect, persuade each of its members to act on that principle—this without becoming dictatorial herself or himself? How do we represent public education's "outside" world to our constituency? Is there an implied hierarchy in any group that includes both adults and children, and where might the restraints on older and younger be? And so much more.

That the essays that follow were once letters provides authenticity, large thoughts behind small acts in the daily keeping of school. By reissuing them just as they were written we hope to attract a new, larger group of readers than just "our" families, ones who might thereby be reminded that the often strained but never dull raising and learning up of children and adolescents is a task best tackled together by families and teachers that understand, respect, and collaborate with each other.

# A History of the Mission Hill School

*Deborah Meier*

Started in the fall of 1997, the Mission Hill School was designed for kindergartners through eighth graders as part of a systemic initiative to give public schools greater freedom and flexibility. It thus offered a chance to create from scratch a school on the model of Central Park East (CPE) in East Harlem, which had been the center of my life for so many years; this time I had considerably greater freedom as well as a chance to rethink old ideas. On the other hand, it was a time of impending state and national mandates aimed at standardizing schooling, and that soon posed serious dilemmas for the initiative.

From the start, "habits of mind," schoolwide curriculum, and graduation by external review pioneered at Central Park East Secondary School (CPESS) were translated into an elementary school setting without losing the qualities of playfulness, personal engagement, and caring that characterized CPESS's approach. Mission Hill sought, in this new time and place, to show how a small community with substantial local authority could respond to the demands of a larger public urban system. We sought explicitly to create a setting—as we declared in our mission statement—that honored as much as it could what we knew about how children learned, what sustained a strong community, and how to inspire a lifetime love of learning, fairness, and the spirit of democratic life. Lofty ambitions to attach to such an intimate little struggling community! But having ambitions articulated in this way helped us then—and continues to help us now—in innumerable, practical ways.

We began with one hundred kids and grew to our permanent size of 175, sharing an old tall-ceilinged, large-windowed former Catholic high school building with an equally small public high school. The building, located in Roxbury, was leased and later bought by the city for our joint use. The students and their families are mostly of color—mostly African American. The remaining students are about equally divided between families describing themselves as Latinos and whites, plus a few Asians. A slight majority are sufficiently low-income to qualify for free or reduced lunch. Half the kids live within walking distance of the school and half are bused in, a ratio that is based on the design of Boston's assignment policy.

The kids come to us through a lottery system, originally intended to foster racial integration, and we have no say over who enters—except that families must visit us before their child's acceptance is final.

We are part of a Pilot network, which means, by agreement of the Boston Teachers Union and the Boston Public School system, that we, along with nearly twenty other Boston public schools are exempt from most union rules and many of its protections. We have greater freedom in hiring staff, deciding on curriculum, and designing standards and assessment tools—except for state-mandated tests. Pilot schools receive the same per capita funds but are given greater flexibility and authority on how to use them. One of the advantages of such flexibility, for example, was our ability to have co-principals.

Of course, the staff have joined voluntarily too, rather than being assigned, and that includes agreeing to be part of a school that rests on community—an oh-so-time-consuming model. The core faculty are paid extra to "think like a principal" as well as like classroom teachers, to be authorities not only in their classrooms but in the larger community. This includes a commitment to five extra hours of collective time together each week and an additional three weeks over the summer. Each student graduates based on collectively decided criteria, and all are accountable for the results.

From top to bottom we are mutually accountable, responsible for each other's work. Kids graduate based on a portfolio system (future letters home will explain this), which requires participation by every member of the staff and each child's family participates when the crucial time to exhibit the student's work arrives. We think this structure of mutual responsibility is critical not only for the comfort of the staff—in fact it's often *uncomfortable*—and not only because it improves our teaching, but because it is the framework for teaching kids about what taking responsibility means in a democratic community, how democracy works (and sometimes doesn't), and what skills and dispositions it calls upon us to display. It thus seeks to align our view of the purposes of public education with our pedagogy, curriculum, assessment, and governance.

The school, not just the collection of individual classrooms, is the central unit of learning at Mission Hill. For instance, the decision to have a schoolwide curriculum means that in any given year five-year-olds and thirteen-year-olds are studying the same themes at the same time. The themes come around again, so students immerse themselves twice, once when they are little kids and again when they are our big kids.

The newsletters, which go out weekly, are one place where the school as a whole shares ideas, events of last week and those coming up, children's writings, and much else. It's where we probe the themes we're studying and how they fit into the larger goal of the school. The newsletters are sent out on Mondays along with a letter from each classroom teacher (children stay with the same teacher for two years in multiage classrooms), homework suggestions or assignments, and occasional parent-organized newsletters and flyers. They are one of the many ways—none of which ever seems enough—that the school tries to keep in touch in a predictable way with its community. The letters are written as much for the staff as for families, and they are debated and discussed at staff meetings. Particularly sensitive ones are usually shared ahead of time with the staff for comments and critiques. Since the summer of 2002, the weekly columns are alternately written by co-principal Brian Straughter, and occasionally columns appear from other staff members or on occasion by students. (The story of Mission Hill's founding and culture gets told in greater detail in *In Schools We Trust*, Beacon Press, 2002.)

In the spring of 2003, the third class of graduates moved on to high school. Some students chose to leave before eighth grade for other, more selective schools. But the vast majority graduated and faced an increasing array of public high schools, charters, private or exam schools from which to choose. Our graduates mostly moved on at the "right age" and got into their top choices. So far the data suggests that far fewer have had to repeat a grade than is typical of Boston students, and as yet none has dropped out. More data will take years to assemble; but as the kids come back to school often to tell us about their lives, we're feeling pretty confident about what the future will show.

# On Keeping School at Parker

*Nancy Faust Sizer*

When Ted and I first started our careers over forty-five years ago, our only real problem with public schools in general was that they didn't have us as teachers. Sure, they were in need of partial reform—more science, perhaps, or greater attention paid to the children of the poor—but the basic ideas in school-keeping (hours spent, age-grading, comprehensiveness, certification, tests, report cards, school districts) seemed pretty impregnable. We wouldn't have believed then that people like us would help to "found" a public school when there was already one in the district. Yet in 1994 when a few of our friends were eager to take advantage of the new Massachusetts Charter Law to create an Essential school in our own neighborhood, that is exactly what we did. And it has been one of our major interests—some might call it an "obsession"—ever since.

The Francis W. Parker Charter Essential School is thirty miles northwest of Boston in central Massachusetts, a fascinating region of rolling hills and distinct towns: not quite suburban, not quite rural, somewhat influenced by the hardships of nearby old textile cities that are trying to find a new industrial base. Since Parker was a start-up, there was a school to design and procedures to outline before our request for a charter was approved by the state. Once we had the charter, there were students and teachers to gather, furniture to find, and much more planning of how we would all work together. As our obligations to other educational institutions were cut back, we moved back into the area fulltime, and as "founding trustees," we took part in all those activities.

In its first year, 1995–1996, Parker was filled with "founders": 120 "founding students," many sets of "founding parents," 15 "founding faculty and staff," about 10 "founding trustees." Recruiting students had been tricky: at first we had no building, no principal, only the beginnings of a faculty. The atmosphere was yeasty, chaotic, sometimes disappointing, sometimes exciting beyond our wildest dreams. Our future seemed fragile, always subject to the whims of the legislature and the trust that students and their parents were able to put in us. At the beginning, at least half of our students were running away from an already existing school rather than running to us. Some of our students came reluctantly, since it was their parents' idea, not theirs. Most were won over, but not all, and each time a student left we worried about the stability of our school. But by the end of the year, when we realized that we had actually created something, it made for a bonding among all the founders that continues to be strong.

Because there was so much to do, Ted and I were at the school often, and we knew the school well. We appreciated its hard-working and idealistic trustees, its young and buoyant faculty, its friendly students and its brave parents. We were all risk-takers, although we each had different stakes in case we fell on our faces. During its first years as an underfunded school in a dreary office building, Parker didn't attract these pioneers with promises of laptops or a magnificent library. Rather, they were attracted by ideas: those that Ted had put forth in his books and in the Coalition of Essential Schools and, as we developed, other similar and imaginative ideas of its founding faculty, trustees, and parents.

What exactly were our ideas? Predominant among them was the notion that adolescents can use their own minds joyfully and well as long as their school is primarily devoted to that purpose. Parker's conversation—but also its organization and its budget—stresses high standards and a deep curricular reach, but also a small number of students for each teacher; careful, individual attention for each student; promotion based on work done and mastery achieved rather than time spent by its students; and a community of all-purpose builders rather than isolated specialists. These are alluring proposals even when they lie quietly on the pages of a book; they are even more exciting when, bit by bit, they are actually brought to life.

Although we had been—and continue to be—gathered by ideas such as these, Parker people have also found great purpose in creating a new school with each other. In an old deserted army base, in a brick building that had once been used for highly secret military intelligence and thus lacked windows, and from families in more than forty surrounding towns, we were creating a new institution and a vibrant community. Parents worked in the office, assisted our teachers, came to meetings, joined the faculty and the trustees. When it came time to decide what academic work our junior high schoolers would need to be able to do to go on to our high school, we invited parents and community members to help to define our standards. Together, in an atmosphere of colleagueship, we made judgments about real, though unidentified, student work. Those of us who were teachers found that our assessments were surprisingly similar to those of the parents. To this day, whenever I think of what the word "community" really means, I think of those early meetings.

What difference did it make that we were a charter school? For us, a charter school was a valuable, even crucial means, but not an end. In the Massachusetts law, a school proposed what it wanted to do and how it would know whether it had done it; if the state agreed with its plans, it awarded the school a charter. It then funded the school depending on how many students enrolled in it and what the towns from which they came spent on their public schools. No town sent us money along with the child to educate; instead, money that might otherwise have gone to his home town's system (based on its spending per pupil) came to us directly from the state. We got more money if the students came from well-funded towns; less money from the less well funded towns; more money from high school districts; less from K–12 districts; and we never knew exactly what our budget would be until we analyzed the lottery and determined exactly who would be with us in a given year. A few of our students came from home schooling or from private schools; in effect, these were people who were reentering the public sector. We got no help from the state for buildings, transportation, or a cafeteria. Although the intricacies of charter law were and remain of great concern to us, what was most important to us was our ultimate goal of being a successful Essential school.

If being part of a brand new Essential school was welcome but unexpected, it was an even bigger surprise—to us and to others—that we served jointly as its acting co-principals a few years later. We were supposedly retired. In the spring of 1998, however, when as trustees we were looking for interim leadership, we suddenly looked at each other and thought, "Why not us?" No matter how much gray hair we had—or were likely to get in such an undertaking—we knew we could last for a year. Moreover, we could split the responsibilities, help the school to survive a number of important inspections and hold the fort as noncandidates while the community took the time to decide what kind of leadership it wanted. For both of us, schools are vital and fascinating places to be, and "keeping school," in whatever form it takes—teaching, answering the phone, sweeping up—is The Work of the Lord. Ted had been a principal before; and I, a career history teacher with a certain skepticism of administration, was eager to see what the job was really like.

By the summer of 1998, in its fourth year of operation, Parker's students were three hundred strong, ranging in age from twelve to seventeen, chosen largely by lottery, although siblings of students already in the school had an advantage. Socioeconomically and academically, our students tended to bunch in the middle rather than on either end. Most teachers were on the young side, fortified with interns; others were merely young in heart, like us. We had about forty teachers for three hundred students, a very generous ratio, and clearly where we chose to spend our money. Parents were crucial members of our team of builders. Our first three Founders—the Founders who got a capital letter—were parents, and parents have been our philosophers, our recruiters, our teachers, our advocates, our supporters ever since. Most of all, they have been our students' parents, and to play that role many of them have had to learn about, and endorse, a new educational philosophy, even a brand new language about learning. To help them in that crucial task, since the beginning of the school, a package of announcements has been sent home every week, with a cover letter that keeps the parents informed about what is on the leader's mind. In this, Laura Rogers and Jim Nehring, our predecessors as leaders, were inspired by Deborah Meier, who had written such letters to the families in her schools for years. In that way, the events of the week were used to illuminate—and to develop—the school's philosophy. Reading those letters had been of great interest to us during Parker's first three years. Now it would be our turn to write them, and we looked forward to the challenge.

# PART I
# Learning

# Learning

## TURNING LESS INTO MORE

*Nancy Faust Sizer*

During the year that we were acting co-principals, a parent came up to me in the hall and said that she was delighted by the class that she had just observed. "It was fun, and the kids seemed really into it. My child actually spoke a few times!" But then her face grew a little wistful. "I didn't see a lot of notes being taken. What do you suppose they are really learning?"

It is an important question, and I wasn't surprised that the parent seemed confused—even worried. Making decisions about a child's schooling is one of a parent's biggest jobs, and since most parents went to very different schools from Parker or Mission Hill, they have a different notion of what "school" means. To communicate well, we need to begin with what their experiences and their opinions may be. One way to explain our ideas about the best ways to approach learning is in terms of what it *is not*.

As startling as it may sound, we believe learning *is not* primarily the transfer of information by adults who know it to children who do not. Of course, we insist that our adult staff be well prepared for the work they need to do and that they have an interest in and some background in what they're teaching. But we also want to hire people who are prepared to recast what they know into different formats so that their knowledge can be accessible to new and different learners. We also need teachers who are willing, if necessary, to dive into areas that are new to them. This might well mean learning new things—such as the wide range of ancient civilizations, as discussed in one of these letters—alongside the students who are learning too. What makes it necessary to move in an uncharted direction? A child has shown interest, which is a fundamental building block toward learning.

We also believe that learning *is not* primarily furthered by attentive listening, note-taking, memorization, and performance on tests. Although some listening is obviously helpful for students, most of them need air time themselves as they sort through their own reactions to new ideas and new information. They also need to actually work with those ideas and that information in projects that are carefully constructed to advance the initial learning. And, wherever possible, they need to add their own choices, ideas, talents, and style to their work, just as the more successful of them will be able to do in the real world.

Learning *is not* efficient. All the techniques in the world will not teach a roomful of third-graders or ninth-graders how to spell twenty words in a short amount of time. Some of them will already know how to spell them, so they will get bored and restless. Others will lose confidence if asked to do it alone; still others will struggle even after they have been helped, cajoled, threatened. The human mind can be mysterious at times, and it is our business to understand it, one mind at a time. Parents, being parents, understand that last point; efficiency often fails at home too. But they hope that it is different for us since we are teachers and are experienced and trained for our jobs. And parents are taxpayers too, so they would like us to be able to work miracles in that respect.

Mission Hill and Parker needed to erase these and other traditional visions of what learning actually is from our parents' and students' heads and replace them with new hopes for what school might be. Learning is different in our schools. It requires the creation of an atmosphere of purpose and respect. The tone might be serious, but it is not harsh. It requires knowing each other, taking time, allowing children to enjoy their progress and "own" their work. Most of all, it requires turning what might be considered to be "less" in a traditional schoolroom into what would be appreciated as "more" in the context of a person's whole life. "Less is more" is one of the principles of the Coalition of Essential Schools. The motto usually refers to choosing depth over coverage, but in a way it speaks more broadly to the approach we take to learning.

What is less at Mission Hill and Parker, and what is more? For one thing, less is the number of students: Fewer in the schools, fewer in the classes, fewer for each teacher to know well, and fewer classes in a day. This is crucial, because what is more is the time each teacher will spend with the child, the range of subjects to be taught in a class, and, therefore, the extent to which each student will be known. Sharply decreasing the number of students means students do not go by in a blur in our schools. They come in relatively small numbers, they are shared among adults, and they stay a while. Considerable time is set aside during the school day and the school year for the conversations with students and their parents or guardians that are so crucial to knowing someone well.

Yet even with those carefully constructed advantages, the demands on teachers are not less, but different. A teacher "studies" her students; she is expected to know what her student is good at, in and out of school; what his home is like, and the dreams and support that he gets there; who his friends are, and the ways in which his friendships affect his schoolwork. A teacher, who is often also an advisor, looks into each child's history as a student in different subjects. By doing so she learns how he acquired mastery over a skill or a body of information and how he handles setbacks. The teacher then devises and tests—and redevises and retests—new methods for making the student more successful in his work. Having fewer students can be an awesome responsibility. Some teachers take to the new demands and the new environment, and some do not.

A focus on building a few crucial skills permeates and directs the curriculum. On the whole, students can see the point: it makes them feel more powerful. They may not like the book a teacher has assigned, but they do want to be better readers. They may find it difficult to write a particular essay, but they feel proud when others have understood and admired their writing. For years, Ted has stressed "getting the incentives right," and by this he means that if teachers and their students want the same thing, they will be seen as teammates, not adversaries. Teachers do not strive toward certain goals while students work toward others; instead, they consolidate their goals. What emerges is another principle of the Coalition of Essential Schools: "student as worker, teacher as coach." Basically, the students, from the youngest right on up, do want to be workers—as long as they are successful workers. And as their own sense of agency increases, it improves the atmosphere in the school.

Besides skills, we want to instill habits; but, again, we start with only a few in each school. Deborah has five simple questions that she expects her students to be able to answer, such as "How do we know what we know?" and "Who cares?" These are not as simple as they seem, if really tackled. In the same way, Parker has designated eight basic "habits of learning," such as curiosity, organization, and involvement. In a poster in every classroom, each habit of learning is described in two or three sentences. For example, the description of involvement states "Both in school and in the larger community, you take the initiative to participate in the process of learning. You contribute your questions, ideas, and actions in group discussions, activities and projects." With these and other rubrics developed for work in academic areas, expectations are specific and much discussed. Students tend to be knowledgeable about their strengths and weaknesses in each of the academic areas and the habits of learning, because they are seen against the backdrop of a student's whole career—even the student's whole life.

Much of the "less is more" philosophy rests on our belief that doing something thoroughly and well is more likely to lead to mastery and enjoyment. Thus the number of topics to be studied in a given year is fewer. This is obviously extremely hard to do—there are so many worthwhile things to study!—but we hold to our principles as diligently as we possibly can. At Mission Hill, as one of these letters indicates, much time might be given to the study of snails. Not every child would be equally fascinated, but every attempt would be made to share the wonder in these creatures: they would be touched, described, plotted over space and time. Attempts would be made to learn how they eat, reproduce, fit into their context, and what kind of context is best for them. Even for those who would rather study—for example—gears, the unit on snails has introduced them to the experience of focus, depth and the way those qualities can lead to engagement—even passion. At Mission Hill, they also repeat schoolwide themes when students are older in order to emphasize the fascination and joy that can come with greater maturity and new investigations of a familiar topic.

At Parker, an analogous unit might focus on a certain historical period in Mexico that dominates the Arts and Humanities curriculum for a couple of months. Classes read a novel and historical texts; they study and practice the art and music of the era; they use their Spanish, which is studied by all students; and they take carefully prepared trips to nearby museums and other local places of interest. The number of books to be read in such a unit may be few, but the book is read very carefully. Assignments may be built around it. If the book is a novel, students may be asked to write new endings preserving certain aspects of the original characterizations, or they may be asked to construct dialogues or draw pictures that illustrate crucial events or states of mind.

Once the students know a text well, they can discuss it with confidence. They enjoy the fact that they see it differently than other students do. They feel more alive as they assemble the facts that will support their own theories. By allowing their students to delve into a few sources rather than to whiz through a number of them, teachers are accepting them as people who can develop something to add to the interpretation. The students are respected. The emphasis is not only on their longstanding interests and biases, though, but on the new interests and opinions that may develop in the course of doing hard work. This work can be done at home or at school; again, less is often more. At Parker and Mission Hill there is a real attempt to avoid homework-for-homework's-sake. Both Ted and

Deborah wrote letters on this tender subject, emphasizing the point of doing the homework that we do have, both for school and for the habits necessary for the responsibilities that lie ahead.

One dilemma we face when constructing curriculum is balancing our desire to keep it simple while also following our students' interests. Considerable experience has made us good predictors of what topics—snails? or gears?—will attract them, but we need to look carefully at each new group we teach and adapt accordingly. A typical class is two hours long and has in it a range of talents, predilections, and ages. Thus our assignments and projects may well vary, not only in the level to which we are asking an individual student to aspire, but also in the communication methods he may use and the parts of the topic he will investigate. Classes are organized into units, not year-long surveys. The students know less about the War of 1812 than in other schools, but often more about the literature, music, art and history of the Civil War. Thus, there is considerable choice in content—a real challenge for teachers—but there are also essential skills that need to be mastered, which can be a real challenge for some students. Various workshops are offered for those students who need more practice or who take extra delight in certain skills. But a student is not allowed to work only on what she naturally gravitates toward. Variety in our requirements, honesty in our teachers, and self-monitoring in our students keep them working at what they like less as well as what they like more. We can handle all this variety because a teacher's daily schedule includes two hours devoted to planning classes, most often with colleagues.

Over time, with larger assignments and older students, the progression is toward more and more independently designed assignments. Parker reserves electives only for its oldest students. But even while working with electives, students must convincingly demonstrate mastery of the electives' skills in their graduation portfolio. There may be only a few qualities of mind that are considered crucial for earning the diploma, but these qualities and the skills that support them are practiced, practiced, practiced. We want our students to have faith that when they go to their new environment they will have what it takes to succeed there, as long as they are prepared to work hard.

How hard do our students work? Harder than they think, since they tend to like and trust their taskmasters. By linking promotion to a student's own performance, we are putting our children through their paces all the time. Every day matters; assessments are an integral part of learning and are built into every activity. At Mission Hill, there are frequent opportunities for students to show what they are learning. At Parker, a "Challenge of the Week," affectionately referred to as a "COW," summarizes a week's work in math and science in the Division I, but also leaves room for a student's imagination. To my practiced schoolteacher's eye, it seems "cheatproof," as are the rest of our assignments, because so many of them are tailored to a student's own interests and working style. We don't rely only on our own impressions but are likely to ask the students frequently what worked for them to get closer to mastering a skill or understanding a body of knowledge. In our schools, like others, assessment can be stressful. To be told that more practice is necessary or that one's theory is not convincing or even that one is not ready to move to another division feels quite shattering—even "high stakes."

Still, there is less emphasis on the experiences in school that have profoundly intimidated students over the centuries. There are, for example, fewer tests in our schools, which enhanced recruitment efforts during our time at Parker. Instead, assignments can be varied; time is provided; sources are adapted if they prove to be an unreasonable stretch. Most important, the opportunities to revise important assignments are more numerous than in other schools. The emphasis is on growth, on learning from one's mistakes, cleaning up one's prose, clearing up one's understanding. Like athletes, students need to want to perform well, and they need to respond to the person who is helping them to become stronger and more competent. They need to be able to listen not just to praise but also to criticism and advice. It's not an easy form of listening, for any age, yet it is a crucial skill to attain.

Some teachers fear that revision gives some students more time than other students have, and thus an unfair advantage. But advantage over what? Until I began to see learning differently, I used to feel nervous about giving extra time for some students or offering the opportunity for rewrites. (Yes; I taught in traditional schools, and I gave tests—hard ones, in fact.) I was so afraid that I might be unfair—or that I might be seen as unfair. But after a while I came to believe in the simple fact that learning is more than competition. It is what the whole process is supposed to be about. Letting Susie take more time to complete an assignment is not going to make Sally learn any less. They may sit next to each other in the same classroom and they may, in fact, have a good deal in common, but what's going on in each one's head is likely to be quite different. In fact, for little children and even for the high schoolers, we believe that competition harms the motivation to learn more than it helps it, so we discourage it in our two schools. It would be pretty hard to get rid of it entirely, but to a remarkable extent, we have been successful.

There are limits to extra time and to revision, however. After absorbing one's coach's advice, it is still the student who goes out to play the game. At Mission Hill, the student eventually reads aloud without correction, all on her own, and her reading is taped, saved, and used when decisions need to be made. At Parker, a student is not considered ready for the final Division III in Arts and Humanities until she can devise and complete a substantial assignment with only minimal help. However collaborative our atmosphere, however long it may take, the earning of a diploma needs to be seen—and experienced—as an impressive individual accomplishment. Only then will our graduates have the confidence that they will need to achieve in the next phases of their lives. We want them to miss us but not because they have grown dependent on us.

There is a true story that has haunted me for years about a teacher in the 1930s who said to his students, "I don't care what you think about Wordsworth. What I care about is whether you remember what I think about Wordsworth." We would not be so blunt today, but we are still too often preempting the students' own ideas and passions with the teacher's "one best answer." At Parker and Mission Hill, learning is constructed differently. The slow, methodical development of the students' answers to their own or others' questions is more likely to stay in their minds. Even if after a while they don't remember details, they remember the process they went through and the respect that was shown to them as they went about what increasingly felt like their own work. They remember their own progress—or lack of progress—particularly in the area of time management. And learning how to do a piece of work well was its own reward, which is not to say that they didn't bask in the praise that they were given when the time came to exhibit their work to a variety of others!

The letters in this section are our answers to the parent who asked, "What do you suppose they are really learning?" Our students are learning not to be afraid of learning. They are learning that school can be interesting, even fun. They are learning that engagement can come in many guises, but that it's greater when one actually takes part. They are learning that working hard is fine, even expected, but that being uninterested leads quickly to being uninteresting, and is definitely to be avoided—all through one's life, and especially at school.

# The Letters on Learning from Mission Hill

### ON SNAILS

*The first curriculum that the school got involved in happened by accident. Since we were starting a new school, we had thought that studying our neighborhood would be a good idea. We had lots of grandiose plans, and some of them got carried out. But, in fact, what really captured us all was the unexpected infestations of land snails we found everywhere around the schoolyard! There's never been anything like it since, so I don't know how to account for it. And then one thing led to another. It brought home an old truth: being interested is the starting point. It was a lucky accident of our history that land snails galore were as fascinating to five-year-olds as they were to sixty-five-year-olds.*

Dear Families, Students, Staff, and Friends,

A *Time* magazine reporter called; she asked me what we were studying. I told her "snails." She got very enthusiastic and told me her son had studied snails and somewhere she thought he had a booklet he had written about them that she'd send us. She told me all about their hibernating habits. We built a fast rapport. One can never tell where snails can lead.

What's the difference between a seed, a pit, and a bulb? Kids are planting bulbs in our front yard; we're also negotiating for a garden on Parker Street for future vegetable gardening.

Reading all the class letters is wonderful. We'll post them outside the office so that all can see what each class is doing and learning, along with the homework teachers and students have invented: learning new and odd words, memorizing poems, writing family books, making maps, doing math puzzlers, etc.

A famous mathematician and computer whiz at MIT named Seymour Papert wrote an essay about his early love of gears. He said he entered into those gears with a passionate personal identification. That made me think about our habit #1—stepping into the shoes of others. Sometimes we can even step into the shoes of objects and plants—not just people or animals. Lifetime hobbies and careers are often built out of strong love affairs with living and nonliving things that other people think mundane, boring or of only practical interest. Papert commented that he was lucky that there were adults around who didn't judge him by test scores but by his real life intelligence as applied to the things in life he loved.

Researchers interviewed students at my old NYC school ten years after they had graduated. The graduates listed as the school's most important asset that it had nurtured and extended their personal interests and points of view. It was those special interests that were at the heart of their later school and life success. (The other secret of the school's success, said the graduates, were the relationships they built with others during their school lives. More on that next week.)

As we meet with families this fall to talk about your children, let's commit ourselves to looking together at what each child's special way of seeing the world might be and how together we can nurture it—as well as the relationships they're building with others.

—DEBORAH MEIER, *October 14, 1997*

## THE MIRACLE OF READING FOR PLEASURE

*Book lovers have learned one special skill: to enjoy the adventures of other people, other times, and even other species, to thus add many lifetimes to our own. Too often, in the push for increased literacy, we focus on reading directions, or getting information—necessary, we claim, for success on the job (or in school). We too often ignore the power of a good story to expand our too-short lives tenfold—and not just in kindergarten. It's that ancient, fundamentally human love of a good story that is the biggest pedagogical tool we have for teaching reading. Like budding basketball players, a lover of reading can throw baskets morning, noon, and night. This was written as a plea for more reading-aloud at home and less worrying about when the child starts reading on his or her own.*

Dear Families, Students, Staff, and Friends,

Why read? Well, it's important for passing courses and tests in school. According to some other recent pronouncements, its other big value lies in being able to follow directions on labels. Big deal.

Reading printed words is what I'm talking about. It's good to remember, however, that we also "read" people's faces and gestures; pictures, movies, and TV shows; and numbers. Learning to read in these other ways is part of having a good and successful life too.

It has been said that aside from providing information—what's in the bottle, what day it is, who won the game—reading offers us extra lives. It allows us to have more than one lifetime's experience. Through reading we can become many different people and visit different places—past, present, and future—even places that have never existed and never will!

Reading lets us step into the shoes of an old man or woman, or a young child, to feel what it might be like to be another animal, to have lived at another time, to have been born another nationality or race or gender. We laugh and cry experiencing new worlds and new friends. Stepping into the shoes of all these people leads us to learn naturally about what they knew. All kinds of factual information as well as visual images become part of us.

We can argue with people we'd never otherwise meet and learn about viewpoints that no one we know has ever mentioned to us. We learn things that allow us to reach our own conclusions about whether what the headlines say or what the TV announcer or ad says is true. We can, if we choose, become self-educated experts in all kinds of things.

None of this can happen if we don't learn how to read. But just knowing how is not enough. We must become true readers, virtuosos, addicted to the written word. That's what we call Level 7 reading at Mission Hill.

Reading may occasionally have to feel like work (Levels 5 and 6). For some unlucky people it may almost always be that way. But for most of us reading can become play—the reading itself requiring no effort at all. At this level, the effort is in working and playing with the ideas themselves, engaging with the author and the world the author has brought to us. The new ideas and experiences can be painful, can require us to stop and think deeply; they can also bring enlightenment, offer good advice, or change our lives.

For some kids, it happens in first grade. But later is fine. Last week a student told me that at age thirteen she has just "discovered" reading. She knew *how* to read long ago. She even does okay on tests, but she never read a book for pleasure, until now. She has a lifetime ahead to indulge her newfound hobby.

Such miracles are what we live for here at Mission Hill.

—DEBORAH MEIER, *October 2, 2000*

## WERE YOU GOOD TODAY?

*What kids make of the fact that they are required to spend years and years in school—a truly new event in the history of humanity—is of importance to us all. The answers kids give are often sad. Trying to help parents see how they play into the bad answers—not to mention how schools do the same—was the point of this letter. What are the messages we adults send to kids about schooling? Do we tell them it's where they are going to have so much fun finding the answer to so many questions that they have? Public opinion polls consistently show that more parents say they judge a teacher or school based on whether their kids are enjoying themselves. More than anything else, parents mention how important it is that their children enjoy their school, and they rank that enjoyment as much more important than test scores. So it's worth pushing this point: they're right.*

Dear Families, Students, Staff, and Friends,

When I first began teaching kindergarten I often dropped kids off at home at the end of the morning (I didn't teach afternoons at that time). I noticed that the first thing parents asked their children was "Were you good today?"

I soon found that when the parents came to conferences at school the first thing they asked me was whether their children had been good.

I asked the children, "What do you think is the main reason parents send their children to school? What do they want you to learn here?" Almost without exception they answered, "To learn to be good." It fit.

So the next question was "What does 'being good' mean?" The kids were clear: being quiet, raising your hand, getting in line properly, taking turns, not talking out, not hitting. Not a bad list of virtues for living together in school, but not exactly inspiring to young children. When pressed further about the purpose of school they added learning the alphabet and their numbers, and then learning to read. (Later on they would add learning their multiplication tables!)

Again, these are all quite proper. They might be inspiring except that, on the whole, the kids didn't see any reason to learn these things—except to avoid being "left back" or to earn a diploma. They mostly see reading and knowing one's multiplication tables as "just for school."

But we know that the real drive to become smarter, wiser, and more knowledgeable that starts at birth is the unstoppable need to understand, make sense of things, become a grown-up, and be powerful. Children learn an enormous amount even before they start school because they are driven by a thirst for both mastery and play. They are naturally curious, they love to think, they are philosophers and logicians, artists and designers, makers and doers.

Our school's agenda is based on these goals—on the things kids really want to accomplish and be good at. Then we want to show them that the other kind of "being good"—following the rules of the game—makes learning what really counts a lot easier.

Try asking your kids different questions at home, like "Any interesting questions come up today at school?"

"Did anyone say or do something surprising, odd, unusual, unexpected?" Or just tell *them* about what *you* learned that day—what interesting or surprising questions arose for you. Like "I had a different bus driver today because. . . ." Or "I figured out why Mr. So-and-So is always so grumpy on Mondays. . . ." One thing sometimes leads to another.

And here's a tip for parent conferences: Instead of "Was my child good today?" ask us "Did he surprise you today?"

—DEBORAH MEIER, *September 11, 2000*

## THE WAY WE TEACH

*Despite numerous attempts, we haven't succeeded in answering the question that motivated this column: is Mission Hill tough enough? Some assume we teach the way we do because it's easier. It's not. Some think we're not rigorous enough in our demands. Since rigor means harsh and unbending, we plead guilty—but not to being too soft. We think our five habits of mind are tough to master and that few kids leaving our school (and few of us adults) have mastered them so thoroughly that we always use them in times of stress. But our nine-year curriculum is meant to get kids in certain habits of mind that will be hard to break, even when easier paths offer themselves. We learn good habits best when the rewards that come from learning are foremost in our minds. So we keep hammering away at it.*

Dear Families, Students, Staff, and Friends,

Do you wonder how we plan curriculum—in math, science, history, or literature? Here's a rough description of the process. We start off with an idea, an experience, a time and place, or a problem. We brainstorm among ourselves about where it might take both us and the kids, and then we read up on the subject, find lots of possible materials, and decide how to launch it. Sometimes we brainstorm a way to cap off our study at the end.

As we teach, we look for connections to our children's own questions and interests, and we notice which ideas and activities seem most engaging to the group. No two classes, or kids, are the same. Those five habits of mind are our constant guide. We try always to be sure that each topic of study lends itself to the development of those habits and that we keep pushing everyone to use them. We also try to be sure that as we study a particular topic or phenomenon kids have lots of opportunities to read about it, model it, talk and write about it, and, if possible, measure it. In short, we try to connect whatever they are studying to practical skills, to the basic disciplines of academia, and to their own special interests and talents—their strengths. Equally important, we want them to fall in love with at least some aspect of what we are engaged in. And all the time we provoke, question, and extend—and offer a lot of feedback.

We have an eight-year curriculum plan designed to ensure a balance between important contemporary social issues, the ancient history of various cultures, and physical and biological science. The whole school follows this plan so that we can provide staff and students with a lot more depth and breadth. Each larger theme comes up twice over the nine-year span, which adds more depth and breadth to our studies.

Over the next few weeks, I'll try to explain why we plan curriculum this way. There is research evidence that our method helps develop the kind of intellectual competence, curiosity, and skill that pays off in high school, college, the workplace, and everyday life. We know there are other ways, but we believe this is the most efficient.

Of course, sometimes we also teach traditional lessons within these broad thematic studies, with precise objectives that all kids focus on, such as memorizing key words or geography terms. And we study topics specific to reading, writing, and math at times set aside for these narrower subjects. Even then, we aim for a balance between a thematic approach and specific directed teaching.

We're going to organize study groups to read and talk about this way of teaching and learning so that those who'd like to can become more expert. At the heart of our philosophy is the importance of asking good questions—so don't be afraid to ask them.

—DEBORAH MEIER, *January 29, 2001*

## A LITTLE HISTORY

*I know parents have occasional twinges of doubt about our Mission Hill way. No textbooks? No individual desks? Not always correcting every mistake? All this attention to relationship building? So this was a letter that tried to review an important principle at Mission Hill: Each Mission Hill parent is a teacher, and a good one. Each one possesses important knowledge and wisdom and knows her own child well. Maybe schools have more to learn from how parents "teach" than the other way around. School is a way for a busy society to do what parents from the beginning of time have done, only we have to try to do it more efficiently because we have more kids and less time! If we want to be nostalgic about schooling in the good old days, we'll have to go back a very long time ago—when all kids were home schooled.*

Dear Families, Students, Staff, and Friends,

I started teaching as a substitute in Chicago forty years ago, when all was supposedly well in America. That experience inoculated me against false nostalgia for "the good old days."

Chicago schools of that era were dead ends for kids, off-limits for parents. One had to respect the sheer stamina of kids and teachers who came back day after day for more boredom, yelling, and meanness.

The schools were traditional to the core. Teachers followed the textbooks while kids sat in rows and maybe listened and filled in answers. The results—both test scores and kids' work (I looked at both)—were awful.

Next I taught kindergarten and Head Start in Philadelphia, then kindergarten in central Harlem. I wrote, read, listened, and observed. My own children were in either the same schools where I taught or the same district, so I listened double—as parent and teacher.

Here's what I learned back then.

Children came to school knowing a lot—no matter how poor or "deprived" their families were. Between birth and six all children, of every race and ethnicity, had learned a remarkable amount of complex stuff. They learned it in the exact same way we learn throughout our lives.

When we started sending kids to school earlier and earlier, we forgot what every mother knows: the most efficient way to learn is not the "sit down and learn" school way—it's the learn-by-doing, hands-on way.

Teaching and learning have always been a part of everyday life and work in the home. Toddlers learn alongside adults and older kids, by natural imitation. They are encouraged to make mistakes; their cognitive errors are not punished, or mocked, or criticized. Their special interests are usually cherished and catered to, and it's taken for granted that they will get smarter and more skillful through experience. Trust is high—on both sides. Schools, many of us thought, could be more like this for all children. They already were like this for those who could afford private school.

Children learn to talk by inventing speech (as I wrote last week), imitating sounds and stringing them together, hoping to be understood. We enjoy their mistakes! We trust to time, a loving home, and encouragement. In just a few years they accomplish a most remarkable intellectual feat, learning their native language, and they continue, on their own, to add about ten new words a day, without any direct instruction.

Such discoveries started me on my way, and helped me (and many others) create schools that produced results few thought possible—for all children. In every respect the schools we have today—and not just Mission Hill—are better and more effective than those of 40 years ago.

—DEBORAH MEIER, *March 17, 2001*

## PATTERNS OF LEARNING

*The fall study of flora and fauna in our immediate neighborhood put the topic of patterns in the center of our work. It's explicit in one of our five habits of mind and connects to virtually everything we study. But this may not seem obviously a wise way to go to parents who often wonder "Why so much time spent on this or that?" So we restate these basic questions—the five habits of mind—over and over. Wouldn't it be grand if together we helped kids see the patterns in their lives—including a few we'd like them to break free of! This letter reached families just six days after the events of September 11, 2001—surely a pattern-shattering day. But over time, maybe we too will see it as part of a pattern and learn from it, rather than just being traumatized by it.*

Dear Families, Students, Staff, and Friends,

The theme of this fall's curriculum focus on nature studies is *patterns*. Sometimes I think we could teach every subject by looking for patterns.

I was walking down the hall the other day, for example, and I noticed that almost every table has a different imitation wood pattern. There are also patterns that occur over time, like the life cycle of the butterfly.

Mathematics is sometimes described as the study of patterns. Discovering the patterns in a number chart thrills some kids. Think about odds and evens, and the patterns in the multiplication tables. Mathematicians have spent centuries trying to discover whether the prime numbers (1, 2, 3, 5, 7, 11, 13) make a pattern. So far, no luck.

Music, of course, consists of patterns of sound. Maybe that's why so many mathematicians are also good musicians.

As we study natural phenomena in each of our classrooms we're looking for patterns. Sometimes we try to impose one on nature. Does that just help us remember, sort, and classify? Is the classification really true to nature? What's the evidence?

Humans seem to be designed to seek patterns, to impose some kind of predictable order on the world around us. Life is too difficult if every event surprises us, or is "out of order." Young children depend on patterns, or routines: waking up, brushing their teeth, hearing a bedtime story. In our classrooms we try to create order and predictability so that we can attend to what is unusual, different, unexpected. Too much disorder makes it hard to focus. But what's too much for one child is not enough for another.

The Mission Hill curriculum is intended to help children look for and find patterns and sometimes invent their own. We study four different ancient civilizations, for instance, helping kids look for patterns across cultures. What's similar and what's very different about the Maya, Egyptians, Chinese, and Greeks? We'll do the same in science, noticing the ways different kinds of scientists look for patterns.

None of this will happen without attending to facts. We can't see patterns if we don't observe closely, and we must take into consideration what others have learned and seen. This means staying with the topic long enough to see where it leads—through observation, sharing, reading, and experimenting.

—DEBORAH MEIER, *September 17, 2001*

## HOMEWORK: THEORY AND REALITY

*The reasoning behind homework is indisputably good. But since we've found it rarely works, we give less homework than most schools. We offer suggestions through the third grade and require less than an hour a night after that. And we keep in mind that if it's to be fair to all kids, the homework needs to be something they can all truly do at home with minimum adult intervention. This was one of many—annual—letters attempting to make our policy sound sensible, doable, and useful. It never ends the issue—some parents want more, some want even less, and some want our "suggestions" to be "requirements," and on and on. We sympathize with both supporters and opponents but haven't found a better solution.*

Dear Families, Students, Staff, and Friends,

Every Monday your child will bring home the school and classroom newsletters and other important notices. Consider them your family homework. Like all homework, it might sometimes be boring. But we'll try to make it as interesting as possible.

This leads me to a confession about Mission Hill and homework: we still haven't figured it out. The theory is that homework serves three purposes: (1) it helps us get to everything that needs doing but can't possibly get done in a mere 5½ hours of school per day; (2) it teaches independence; and (3) it's a way for school and family to keep in touch.

But the evidence shows that homework rarely serves all three, and often it serves none of the above. Sometimes, as one parent said recently, it brings out the worst in everyone. Independent, smart kids show their worst sides to well-intentioned parents, who in turn become ogres. This is hardly a good way for school and family to collaborate. On the other hand, for some kids and some families, homework is a lifesaver.

Best bet: What meets all three goals most often is required reading at home and sometimes reading-related writing tasks. There is no way kids will read as much as they need to if their only reading time is in school. Lots of schoolwork depends on kids having read the assignment ahead of time. And what better way for parents and kids to collaborate than over a good book or article? If the reading gets tedious, what could be better than a family member reading it aloud to a child?

So our number one homework priority is at least 30 to 45 minutes of reading every night. The more the better.

Second best: Some rote tasks can be learned as well at

home as at school: practicing spelling words; memorizing number facts, or poetry. Of course, if the task is too hard, it's not good for home or school.

Finally, there are some activities and games that are better saved for home but are very educational. Almost all card games can be good for practicing math skills; ditto for many board games. Cooking together, making things together, watching good TV shows, doing Internet research together, doing crossword puzzles, playing word games like Scrabble or hangman, drawing, painting, and sculpting are other useful forms of homework. Not to mention genuine work that needs doing at home: washing dishes, doing laundry, etc. And don't forget writing. Wouldn't Grandma appreciate a letter or card?

Every kid is different. But none can learn how to become a grown-up without spending a lot of time in the company of grown-ups. That's homework assignment number one: being together.

—DEBORAH MEIER, *September 10, 2001*

## BOREDOM: A SERIOUS MATTER

*"Bo—or—ing." It's a word I'd like to ban. Kids use it very carelessly, and parents of kids who are quick at schoolwork often use it to avoid looking at bad work habits. It gets in the way of good child/teacher/family communication. Thus this letter home. The trouble is, they are not always wrong, or putting on an act, when they complain about boredom. Schools are mostly boring. And boredom can be a killer. When you're getting bored driv-*

*ing, watch out! Ditto for reading! School works best when we pay attention to what kids (and human beings for that matter) actually can't resist being interested in. Of course, sometimes we're bored with something we'd truly love to learn about, simply because it's too hard. Sometimes because we don't "get it"—yet. My granddaughter now loves art museums—thanks to a wonderful art teacher. But, it's never good to pretend boredom is just one of those necessary things.*

Dear Families, Students, Staff, and Friends,

"Adults rarely pay enough attention to boredom in classroom life," suggests Robert Fried in his new book, *The Passionate Learner.* (Dr. Fried is one of our Northeastern partners.) He says we hear "This is boring" as a "typical schoolboy excuse" for not getting on with one's work. And, of course, sometimes it's just that.

But sometimes it's a misunderstanding about what it takes to become competent. Close observers of children have discovered that, whatever its cause, boredom is not good for learning. In fact, it's a sure sign of not learning. When kids are interested, they are learning (although they might be learning the wrong thing or things we wish they didn't know).

Boredom, then, is a serious matter that we should pay as much attention to as we do disruptive behavior, tardiness, or failure to hand in homework. We can start by taking note of when kids seem bored and when they are interested.

Kids are willing to practice for hours some things,

like shooting baskets, that strike me as boring—at least after a few tries. But some things I can do for hours, like reading science fiction, bore some kids (and some other adults, too). It's normal for individual interests to vary.

Yet we expect that kids should be interested in (and good at) everything schools think is important. Even when we get to college, and surely in "the real world," we organize our lives so that we don't have to be equally good at everything. We pick and choose; and, in fact, the world rewards us for being specialists. Except in school.

What to do? Our job is first to find out what we can about each child's interests. Usually we are interested in things we're good at, but not always. Then we need to see if we can increase the number of things our kids find interesting. That means helping them get better at more things and also getting them into stuff that they never imagined might be fun. (How I wish my grandsons had the same feeling for museums that some of our six- and seven-year-olds do.) It's the best motivator there is: "Wow—that's interesting."

Try making a family chart with lists of what each member is interested in, finds fascinating, or is a fan of. What kinds of books, what section of the newspaper, what kinds of TV shows, what places in the world, which games? Then think about why these things are interesting and how the answers could lead to expanding those interests.

Finally, you can let us share in this family research

work so that we can use the knowledge to make your child a more successful learner of the things we've got to be sure they learn in school.

—DEBORAH MEIER, *October 21, 2001*

WHAT NOT TO TEACH?

*We began with a basic principle: less is more. Better to cover well a few things than to cover everything poorly. But it's hard to resist. First one thing comes along, then another. They each seem so tempting. Occasionally we are saved by a budget crisis or by the ending of a grant. But we need also to be tougher on ourselves and to remember our mission to stay small and simple and to not try to be all things to all kids and families. This letter was the beginning of some tough reconsiderations about what we were trying to do. We'll never resolve this tension between all the stuff we think is important and teaching what's important well. We're likely to go back and forth. (We're fortunate that kids have another sixty years or so to "cover" the rest after they leave us.)*

Dear Families, Students, Staff, and Friends,

We are always getting great ideas. That's in the nature of being human. Lots of them are so good they are hard to resist. But there's a price to pay.

National panels of education experts meet and decide that this or that subject is vitally important and schools ought to teach it. The problem, of course, is finding time to add every new thing to the already stuffed curriculum. The experts solve this problem partly by pushing things to earlier and earlier grades and ages.

As Americans become more aware of other nations' concerns, schools are told to study them. As scientists' knowledge of the universe grows more complex, we're told to start teaching science earlier to get it all in. Everyone thinks his specialty is the most important: how can you call yourself well educated without having studied Asian history, or economics, or number theory, or nineteenth-century literature, or Italian art—not to mention without having studied how to have a balanced diet and do a PowerPoint presentation?

Within each of the major subjects the number of topics that seem "critical" grows and grows. One education research lab did a study of new state curriculum frameworks and concluded that we would have to add nine more years of schooling just to cover all the required topics. The framework writers are only too happy to tell teachers what to add; they never say what to subtract.

At Mission Hill, we try to resist. Our four-year curriculum cycle and our five habits of mind help us focus on what's important within each subject area. But we, too, add, and we don't often subtract. We added string instrument lessons in year two, then hired an art teacher, then added band instruments, then chorus. We've tried various approaches to teaching theater and drama (Urban Improv and now Shakespeare & Company). We added Spanish this year.

But at what price? I'm referring not just to the money these additions cost but the time. When kids are studying any of the above, what are they not studying?

It's not easy to decide what not to teach. It feels awkward, uncomfortable, heartless. Nevertheless, it's time for some hard thinking on this issue. The change in schedule for next year gives us a good opportunity to revisit our priorities. Lots of private schools solve the time problem partly by placing "extras" before and after school, as options, or electives. This forces families to make choices, and leaves the bulk of the already short school day free for the essentials.

The trouble is that one person's extra is another's essential. It won't be easy, but thinking these things out and speaking about them will get us closer to where we want to go.

—DEBORAH MEIER, *January 22, 2002*

# The Letters on Learning from Parker

## HOMEWORK

*We felt that a word about homework early in the academic year was necessary, and we stressed that it was an important means, not an end in itself. Parents play a big role here.*

Dear Families,

"These rows," our teacher said, pointing to our half of my class, "do the odds, one to thirteen. The rest of you do the evens, two to fourteen." So do I remember high school mathematics assignments. Most of us did them, most of the time. We passed them in, got "checked off" and never saw the papers again. I suppose the drill helped us learn. I never really knew. Homework was, simply, grunt work. We complained about it. As a teacher, I assigned homework. "Read the first two chapters, please. We will discuss them tomorrow." If the students didn't do the reading, the class would bomb, with the readers struggling to discuss the matter and the nonreaders faking it or worse.

I like to think that my students ultimately realized why they did the assignments. All of us need to practice what we are learning, from corner kicks to Spanish pronunciation. There is not enough class time to practice well. More time is needed. That's "home" time. And all of us need time for new ideas to marinate. I get an idea, provoked (say) by something I have heard. I need to play with that idea, try it out, fiddle with it. That's most likely done at home. Homework is a means, not an end. For me simply to assign "the first two chapters" unintentionally missed the point. Better that I had told my class that tomorrow we would discuss the introduction of one of the key characters in the novel and that I would query each student on some aspect of the author's introductions of this dramatis persona. (I would even expect them to know what dramatis persona meant.) That is, I would explain the reason for the likely "beyond classroom" work and my expectation of its result.

The end is performance: dutiful homework makes that effective performance possible, whether on a daily assignment or on a long-term project. I cannot imagine Parker preparing its students well for what stretches beyond their graduation without emphasizing the importance of regular and steady work beyond the class hours in Building 2602.

—TED SIZER, *September 25, 1998*

## JOY

*I hoped that the students as well as the parents would read this letter. It is, basically, a justification for hard work in a worthy, and ultimately rewarding, cause. Young people who have never experienced it have never tasted the sweet nectar of independent accomplishment—in a word "joy." (In Parker-speak a COW is a "Challenge of the Week" usually given by mathematics teachers to provoke students to contemplate what is just beyond what they have "covered.")*

Dear Families,

A student recently told us that one of her teachers made class fun. Being an instinctive New Englander, my unspoken reaction was Calvinist. School wasn't for fun. It was to brim with rigorous, demanding, stretching work. (The list of likely severe adjectives has biblical dimensions.) Only by suffering could the important things in life be learned. Only by fear could they be compelled.

Some of us reflected later about these words. "Fun" for me is a day at Fenway Park, even when the Sox lose. Fun is diaphanous, insubstantial. How many care, at least for longer than twenty-four hours, about that Sox score? At the same time, we—of any age—learn poorly when we are bored or threatened. We learn well what appeals to us, what catches our fancy, what inspires us, what brings us joy, what draws us in.

I like the word joy. It is not much used these days, and, if so, in sugary ways. Have a Joyous New Year, the hackneyed greeting card insists. The dictionary tells us that the word means "exultant happiness." For many it is right up there with Fun: meaningless, selfish, even ribald.

The word joy deserves better. I notice with delight the silence that emerges during a formal talk or a play, when the listeners' collective attention is riveted. Something is happening, obviously: people care to listen. I note the "Oh, wow!" comment in a lab: something unseen or not understand comes into focus. I note the intensity of a writer word-processing away, or a soccer player intensely practicing, utterly unaware and uncaring about who might be watching: each is engaged with something he or she cares about. They are taking joy in their work. It means something to them. It does indeed stretch them; it is hard work, demanding rigorous attention. But it is hardly drudgery. It is the excitement of hooking one's mind and imagination around a matter of worthy interest. That's joy.

Teachers at Parker often begin their classes with "starters." These would be called "teasers" in the advertising world, and they are designed to delight their students or to pique their interest. Of course, if a student doesn't know much about a subject, it is difficult to know what will trigger his or her interest. That is why we teachers insist on completed work, even if—at first, at least—its execution is neither fun nor joyful. With growing mastery, however, a student begins to feel the satisfaction of performance earlier not anticipated: the ability actually to converse in Spanish, the quick grasp of the secret of a COW, the pleasing roll of written words in an essay. There is joy in all that. And if there is joy, habit will follow.

—TED SIZER, *November 20, 1998*

## TIME

*By December the shape of the curriculum and its demands were clear to most students and parents. Many worried about their progress. Some parents also worried about why our school spent substantial time on fewer topics than offered in most schools, insisting on revision and review at the expense of "coverage" in the traditional sense, Pocahontas to Admiral Perry by New Year's Day. Our insistence on revision, on getting every bit of work to "meet the standard" before moving on—less is more—is a new approach for many families. We needed to explain its purpose.*

Dear Families,

All teachers struggle with the problem of time.

How long does it take for my students to "get" this previously unfamiliar theorem or event or way of expression? What sort of investment is necessary for them to understand it? To see it in context? To be in the habit of using it when it is called for?

If we devote too little time the students may miss the point, or grasp it superficially, or unintentionally distort it. If we devote too much time, we run the risk of boring our classes and wasting their energies. Confounding the situation is that Student #1 may "get" it today and Student #2 not until next week.

To race over material, with the intention only that the students will be able to identify it on a test given immediately at the end of a unit of work, makes no sense. Quick responses are too often glib and thoughtless: traps that we want to help our students to avoid. Learning must stick to a person's intellectual bones. It must serve that person in any sort of apt future situation, however initially unfamiliar that situation is. Students must learn the value of deliberating, of thinking things through carefully before speaking and acting. That kind of learning can take time, practice and more practice in order to understand the workings of each particular new technique or idea.

Parker believes that less is more, that really understanding something is the necessary condition for being able to use it in the future. It is the habit of using knowledge, and a sure grasp of the knowledge most important to use, that is the ultimate goal. Accordingly, Parker focuses on fewer topics than one sees in most schools, but each in more depth and with a great demand for the use of those topics in new situations. We insist on revision—where the student can appreciate a clear expression of mastery in his or her own work—and we require portfolios where these expressions are retained, ready to remind the student, the teacher, and the parents of earlier important efforts. We know that students proceed at different paces at different times and in different subjects, and our school should be as flexible as is reasonably possible in honoring these varying paces.

All this is easy to advocate but very difficult to do well. Even with all its messiness, however, it is worth the effort. Learning takes time. We must use it as wisely as possible.

—TED SIZER, *December 18, 1998*

## GROWTH SPURT

*Some teachers asked me to write this letter to explain a dilemma they were facing. The policy of a midyear gateway was wildly popular with students and their parents; in fact, some of them would have liked there to be several different gateway times all through the year. For them, the recognition of each individual as unique (as Ted puts it, "No two children are exactly alike") was a chief advantage of Parker. Motivation, interest, a sense of each child's growth were all facilitated by our ability to move each student forward at her own rate. The teachers agreed. For the teachers, however, the midyear gateway itself was problematic—not only for themselves, but for the continuing students in the class, who would face some disruption. The teachers were like shepherds who were trying gently to lead a whole flock to new and higher ground, a journey that requires at least some continuity to feel safe. As a community, we needed to explain ourselves to each other before we could find a compromise. I also referred to the school's "essential question" for the year, which was "Where are the patterns?"*

Dear Families,

I couldn't get over the change in one of my grandchildren during the vacation. He ate his dinner with nary a complaint, then weaseled as much dessert out of me as he could manage, and followed it up with a bowl of cereal! When he asked for another bowl, I could only stare at him. "Growth spurt," he airily explained.

His sister, who is one whole minute older, is on a different kind of growth spurt these days. It concerns the bravery with which she tackles the ski slopes. The two of them also trade off growth spurts in reading and math, in no discernible order and—sometimes—depending on their teachers. They don't expect to develop at the same rate in everything. But they started the year in fourth grade, and they will stay in fourth grade until June.

At Parker, we like to say, smugly, we do better. Each student is invited to progress at his own rate. If her work is solid and thorough, her portfolio and her habits of learning at an appropriate level, she may petition to gateway into a new division in the middle of the year. On that basis, more than one hundred students will change one, two, or even three classes this month. This is a policy of the school that is taken for granted by students and has been strongly endorsed by parents in surveys and forums over the years.

There is another aspect of schoolkeeping, however, which is somewhat compromised by the policy of midyear gateways. It is subtler, harder to explain, but also very important. The classes that start off together in the beginning of the year are small communities. As they gel, and the students and their teachers begin to trust each other, learning increases. The interests, talents, and behaviors of each person become part of a rich blend that usually grows more smooth and functional as the class marches together through a set of experiences and challenges. This learning is slower and less dramatic, but it too is a vital part of our craft.

Where are the patterns? Any school with at least two good ideas in it will sometimes find them to be at odds with each other. In this case, we have decided to honor individual progress over stability and community building in our classes. We recognize, however, that some nongatewayers will be affected by the alterations that we must make to their schedules. We are working to minimize the disruption in every way we can. We will also need your help as counselors so that your children will be able not only to adjust to the changes in their classes but also to understand the ways in which both growth and collaboration fit into the context of our educational philosophy.

—NANCY SIZER, *January 8, 1999*

## DEMOCRACY AT WORK

*This is another explanation to parents, which the teachers asked me to write. It seemed very sensible to the teachers that they have a time during midwinter to update and extend their summer planning. Doing so during the regularly scheduled planning times, during special sessions during the school day, or after school had all been tried, and none was as helpful as a few full days in a row without the diversion of actually keeping school. Sensible as it may have been, however, it also involved change, skiing plans, child care arrangements, and the way decisions are made. Should parents vote on the school calendar? They had done so in the first year. If they were "polled" (which may or may not be the same as voting), should it be at meetings? Through phone calls? E-mail messages? We had a lot to learn about democracy in start-up schools.*

Dear Families,

The Parker Museum of World Cultures, which has been open to admiring observers for the last few days, reminds me once again of the value of faculty planning time. During the summer, it was decided by the Division I teachers that since ancient civilizations, ceramics, and research skills were to be the main emphases in the fall term curriculum, a museum during January would be its best capstone. Six teachers and quite a few parents applied their imaginations and varied experiences to the task. They brought together a number of ideas on how to facilitate the research process. They taught ceramics and curatorship as well as literature and history. They arranged for the students to check out the competition by visiting other museums such as the Boston Museum of Fine Arts and the Metropolitan Museum in New York City. When the exhibits opened, our students were able to display the fruits of their own research and to learn from each other. They were able to find the patterns in the dozens of ancient civilizations that were on display. The museum and last week's MST (Math/Science/Technology) "Exploratorium" were more than any teacher, no matter how skillful, could have done alone. Each was a very complex enterprise, but the large scope, instead of intimidating the students, actually inspired them. In fact, the fall-term curriculum, in every domain, in every division, has been a wondrous and well-crafted endeavor. And it makes Ted and me very proud to be at Parker.

But. *But*. Though the annual academic goals are worked out in the summer, planning in detail for the whole year only during the summer has proven to be difficult. We cannot foresee all that each planning team and student group may need in the latter months of the academic year. The faculty must have larger blocks of time in the middle of the year to do its job well. We propose a schedule for 1999–2000 that reflects that priority. Under our calendar, teachers would plan for three weeks during June and August but would save one week of their planning for the winter. School would start on August 25, a week earlier than this year and similar to some of our neighboring schools. In January, students would have the first week (January 3–7) off, and teachers would come back for intense work on the second term's curriculum. All else would stay the same as this year.

We realize that what's best for the faculty is not always what's best for our students' families, and we welcome feedback on this issue now and at the Parent Forum on February 26. It's quite a feat to design a car and drive it at 60 m.p.h. all at the same time, but that is what we in this new school need to do. We're proud of the hard driving our students and faculty have done this fall and we are determined to continue our 1999 spring-term planning with as much energy and focus as we can muster while school keeps. The proposed adjustment to the 1999–2000 calendar would help us to design next year's curriculum even more fruitfully. We hope you will agree that it's your children who would be the final beneficiaries.

—NANCY SIZER, *January 29, 1999*

## ASSESSING OUR STUDENTS

*Parker students had always taken external tests, but this was our first experience with SATs. Getting into college worried a lot of our students and parents, and for good reason. We didn't play the college "game" the way other high schools did; we didn't rank our kids or construct a curriculum that was likely to feed right into external machine-graded achievement tests. Although our students took their progress seriously, and some were struggling, they were not subjected to high-stakes experiences such as frequent tests, and we reduced fear and competition as motivators as much as possible. Were our students going to be tough enough? Loved too much? We didn't believe that these kinds of tests were completely valid assessments, but we needed to take them, so I saw it as my job to convince the students and their parents that we could meet this challenge too.*

Dear Families,

In a few weeks, our oldest students will turn up in Andover or Dracut or Gardner or Waltham to join their counterparts all over the land in taking the Scholastic Aptitude Tests. Some things never change. When I took my SATs, the most stressful part of all was the trip into the city, finding a place to park, being on time, remembering to bring the "right kind" of sharpened pencils, managing to get to the room on the third floor of the dirty, drafty high school where—praises be!—they had my name on a list.

Other things *do* change, however. When I took the SATs, we were not told our scores. Now, students are not only told their scores, but are even told which questions they got right and wrong. To me, this is a big improvement. Of course, I wish that SATs didn't have to count for so much in our college selection system, but if they are going to count—and for now, they mostly are—then it seems wiser to know more about them.

A student who can analyze her previous mistakes has a big advantage. "Here's what I messed up in the reading comprehension section. I understood the reading passage, but I didn't understand the question I was being asked. I didn't pay enough attention to the 'not' in the middle of the sentence. This means that I need to be wary, because they are going to eliminate the careless. I may have been careless—once. But that doesn't mean that I am not a good reader. I can do better once I really pay attention to what they are asking me to do."

I am full of this internal dialogue these days because I took part in Celia Bohannon's SAT test preparation class last week. Along with Deb Merriam, Beth Kay and Laura Rogers, I learned—a little late, perhaps?—more about what it takes to do well on the SAT. Besides reading comprehension, I learned how to handle sentence completion and even struggled with a few geometry problems. I was particularly proud of my progress in doing analogies after Celia told us to concentrate on what she called the "dictionary definition." There are times and places for creativity, she said, but this is not one of them. Once I understood that, I did much better.

What Celia presented were not "tricks" to memorize. "Tricks" can be forgotten and they only contribute to the sort of ominous mystery that can be the bane of the SAT. What she gave us instead were strategies that make good sense, most of which can be used in other aspects of life. Break down a problem into its parts, each one of which may be relatively simple. Learn ahead of time how certain questions will be cast. Don't try to learn the reading sections; just answer the questions you are asked. Remember that the obvious answer is likely to be correct in the early part of a section, where the problems are easier, but wrong in the latter part. Don't rush, but work steadily, so that you tackle every problem you can. Skip over those that are simply out of the question.

Parents for centuries have given out such good advice. Practice, practice, practice. Learn how to stick to a task for hours longer than you wish you needed. Go to sleep early the night before. Most of all, compare yourself, not with the student next to you who looks so competent, but with yourself in previous tests. And then take pride in your progress.

—NANCY SIZER, *March 5, 1999*

## HABITS

*The end of winter slush, sniffles, and fatigue seemed a good time to remind families that what counted at Parker was not just getting the immediate job done but seeing that "job" as the honing of habits, the long-term, resourceful use of knowledge and skills. School is a means to an end, not (only) an end in itself. Students rarely appreciate this, but their parents or guardians surely do.*

Dear Families,

In every school we think about tomorrow. How good will that essay be? What will be my score on this test? We need also to think about tomorrow's tomorrow, about life beyond Parker, even beyond college if we choose to go there. How will our children or students do in "real life" where the "tests" are unexpected and where no sympathetic teacher or forgiving parent is watching?

It is intellectual habits, not the particulars of subject matter (unless we use them regularly), that are the primary residue of schooling. Deborah Meier, the principal of Mission Hill School in Boston, has written persuasively of what she calls "habits of mind." She identifies five, each cast as a question. From that question, we need to ask other questions.

1. *How do we know what we know?* That is, what is the evidence? How do I know when evidence is good?

2. *Who's speaking?* What is her point of view? What's mine? Does my point of view affect the way I listen to hers?

3. *What causes what?* Where are the patterns and connections? How much do they impose on the randomness of life?

4. *How might things have been different?* Can I imagine two or three alternative scenarios, and what might have made them happen?

5. *Who cares?* Is this topic really important? If so, to whom? Is it still important when it matters to a few but not many?

These questions are deceptively obvious. Taken seriously, they are fundamental and can be applied to many sorts of situations, from academic research and invention to a court of law to figuring out how to untangle some practical problem to sorting out one's feelings in a relationship. They require standing back, looking at context, taking a bit of time, putting some distance between ourselves and the matter at hand. They require restraint and an ability to see a situation from several points of view.

We all admire people who have such habits. They are leaders, creators, inventors, problem solvers. Their judiciousness makes them dependable friends.

As with all habits, habits of mind are difficult to teach and often a boring struggle to learn. They arise from practice, from so much insistence on their use that they become almost second nature. They lie at the heart of a thoughtful life. They are what Parker ultimately cares about.

I commend to you Deborah Meier's book on these

matters: *The Power of Their Ideas* (Beacon Press, 1995). The "they" in her title are students: hers and ours.

—TED SIZER, *April 9, 1999*

## EXPERIENTIAL EDUCATION

*I was asked to give the Costa Rica travel group a little advertising and was glad to do so. For a school with less than its share of money, Parker offered a lot of "field trips." These were not the typical rowdy reward at the end of a school year, but a serious, involving part of the course. Preparation for these trips was greater and more thoughtful than I had ever seen as a student, parent, or teacher. The students were prepared to talk and write about what they had seen and done, and to learn from others' perspectives. They knew what they wanted to get out of the experience and how to tell whether they had been successful, at least in the short term. And despite all there was to do, the whole event was not scripted, because we assumed that such events would also be valuable in the long term and in ways we couldn't always predict.*

Dear Families,

When I was riding in Bus #4 on my way to Shakespeare's *Twelfth Night* on Monday, I thought again about the value of trips and of the great job Parker does in taking them. Too many American schools are not lucky enough to have any travel budget at all. Other schools treat trips as "add-ons," with no real preparation on the students' part or discernible connection to the academic program. But at Parker, an important goal is experience, processed in such a way—usually by speaking and writing—as to give it even more meaning. One of the skills we emphasize, moreover, is processing experience; if all goes well, our students will have developed habits that will lend to their lives the special delight that travel can provide.

Many of Parker's trips spring right from the middle of our curriculum. The performance of *Twelfth Night* was another look at a playwright who has been studied by every Parker student this year. The MST (Math/Science/Technology) trip to Martha's Vineyard last month was planned to be the capstone of the year's work; a dozen activities were provided to help the students answer the trip's essential question. Last year's trip to Ellis Island was at the center of the immigration unit, as were this year's visits to museums in New York and Boston. In Spanish, most of our students have now acted as teachers' aides in a school in Lawrence whose students are largely Spanish speaking. Parker students have taken a combined geology/rock climbing trip, visited graveyards and, quite recently, lost their shoes in the Nashua River!

Besides these curricular trips, the school has sponsored others that are popular, highly educational and led by Parker teachers, starting with their choice blocks. Last year's "trip group" established the practice of taking trips to ready themselves for longer trips; first Boston; then, Washington; finally, Germany. The students learned the skill of money raising and of spending it carefully; of consulting guidebooks and honoring serendipity; of recording their travels in a video and writing thank-you letters. This year's travel groups are continuing many of these good ideas and developing new ones. Parker students studied the Everglades in February, pulled out knickerbeans in Florida in April, and will go to Costa Rica, complete with homestays, in June. (By the way, the Costa Rica travel group's chief money raising event will be a yard sale at the Congregational Church on King Street in Littleton on Saturday, May 15. Come early and buy often!)

And that's not even counting the Sunday River ski trip or the backpacking trip in the White Mountains this weekend. Or the fact that three Parker teachers offered trips back to their alma maters as part of this year's auction! The list goes on. . . .

There's no doubt about it: it would be a lot easier just to stay at home. As a former boarding school house counselor, I know what kind of special fortitude, skill, and love it takes to spend the night with other people's children. Still, I am not surprised that so many Parker teachers have been willing to offer these trips, that they have planned and executed them well, and that have come back to school with tales of learning a lot and of enjoying their students' company. They are that kind of people, and in them we are all blessed.

—NANCY SIZER, *May 7, 1999*

## PASSING "LISTENING"

*One of our fondest hopes is that what students learn in school will reinforce their best habits in daily life. Observing, per-*

*forming, and listening—crucial skills in academic work—are also helpful in other arenas. Hearing a parent say that what his daughter has done in her Division I gateway would have helped him in his work was gratifying, not only to me but to his daughter. What she has shown is authentic, transferable, and gives her confidence that she can thrive as a grownup. Still, at gateway time, even the best of us get a little practical, even reductive; as we fill our portfolios, we may confuse our elaborate preparations for the lifelong habits that are supposed to lie behind them.*

Dear Families,

About a year ago, at a Division II rock climbing/geology field trip where I was acting as a chaperone, a student climbed a tree during the lunch break and seemed impervious to our entreaties to come down. Finally, one of his fellow students thought of a successful strategy. "It's gateway time," he shouted, "and you won't pass 'Listening' if you don't hear us and *come down out of that tree*."

The climber started down immediately, but he was grumbling good-naturedly as he carefully negotiated his passage. "No way am I going to flunk 'Listening,'" he mumbled to himself. "I already have my interviews."

I have treasured that story, retold it often, and carried it around in my heart all this momentous year. It says two things to me about Parker. The first is that our students expect to apply what they learn in school to real-life situations. They realize that listening has academic value, but they also know that it matters in the social transactions that make up so much of life. There's an obvious overlap in the case of listening. But there are also a number of parallels in reading and formal writing, in problem solving and scientific thinking, in the cultural understanding that comes of knowing another person's language. I think that our students and their families know that and respect that part of our educational philosophy.

The second part of the story that pleases me, however, has to do with the quirky way that Parker people think, especially at gateway time. "Listening" for the tree climber took on a rather limited meaning; it was doing his interview, finishing the work required. No matter how often the teachers may have explained that an interview is only one way to demonstrate one's listening skills, this student dealt with it in the way he could: by figuring out what he needed to do to satisfy his teachers. We adults try to describe our requirements as broadly and as philosophically as we can. As often as they can, however, our students remind us that they need jobs fed to them in manageable bites.

It's gateway time at Parker again, and nearly half of our students and even faculty who are facing one or another transition are preparing our portfolios. We are making sure that we are ready to be asked about the work we have done. Like the boy in the tree, we are a little vulnerable, attentive whenever anyone tells us that we may not measure up. No wonder that we get a little mechanical as we count up our pieces.

Transition is hard work, as all you parents of gatewayers must be noticing at home. Ted and I are also getting ready to make our own form of a gateway, as we end this year of deeper involvement with Parker and prepare for a new phase in Parker's—and our own—history. All I can say about the Sizers is that our portfolios are certainly a lot thicker than they were a year ago at this time! We only hope we have enough pieces of "Meets" work to negotiate our own passage with good humor and a modicum of grace.

—NANCY SIZER, *June 4, 1999*

PART II

# Authority

# Authority and Power

*Deborah Meier*

Power relationships have always been a difficult subject for school people to discuss, whether among themselves or with kids or families. "Question authority" was the political slogan of the young in the '60s, at just that time when I first encountered the lifestyle of the traditional public school in Chicago as a substitute teacher and a parent. Public schools were hardly a place of much questioning—of authority or anything else. Parents, particularly if they were poor or black, were largely unwelcome in the schools and seen as an intrusive alternate authority system to be resisted. Despite the existence of a strong union, teachers had little individual say over what or how they taught, or about the daily life of their schools—except behind closed doors. Principals too were constrained by a central board that controlled all matters of importance—budgeting, hiring, curriculum and assessment—although some principals had political alliances that allowed them special treatment. Kids, presumably, were fairly powerless, although I soon discovered that they too had, in their own way, a great deal of power over the way we could or couldn't go about our work as teachers—the power to privately resist and sabotage. (Cumbersome as more open and democratic ways are, in schools as in society at large they have this enormous efficiency—they give the governed an active stake in seeing that things work out.) The results of top-down governance were appalling, but aside from private griping, no one talked too much about authority and power in schools, preferring to carve out their own private spaces. Forty years later, the lines of authority remain pretty much intact in most schools, and the results only somewhat less appalling.

Over the next forty years my colleagues and I consciously engaged in creating schools based on a different conception of power and authority, one consistent with the purposes of democracy and good learning. We wanted a setting in which teachers and kids could both be trusted to do right out of moral and professional conviction and good sense. Our view of high expectations included the expectation that human beings could do so. Still we knew that kids needed the safety of limits and that we were the limit-setters. And we knew that kids needed expertise and that we were the experts. We too were engaged in our own "power struggles" with central authorities—over both expertise and limits. Many of us recognized that the infantilizing of teachers, particularly in K–8 schools, was a major impediment to strong schooling for kids. We focused on pedagogy—how we taught, how we brought kids into a more powerful relationship to their own learning, and on the role teachers played in decision making. Those of us who saw schools as places that could foster the values of a more egalitarian society, a society in which power was more evenly distributed, sometimes forgot that kids were watching us when we weren't teaching too; they were forming ideas about the role of power and leadership, especially as they entered adolescents. How were we to teach lessons inside our classes that we didn't practice or even talk about outside?

Schooling is all about influencing others in ways that increase their independence and autonomy. Whether it's conducting a course on arithmetic or writing, all we have going for us is our capacity to enlighten others in ways that change their own perceptions of numbers and words and ideas—and the way in which knowledge becomes a source of power. Kids are properly attracted to power, and they seek influence. Our modeling of adulthood needed to show them how this might look. Students need to witness powerful adults unafraid to discuss power! (They even need teachers who can discuss race—a topic that is not so far removed from the struggle for power.) Teachers probably are attracted to teaching precisely because they seek influence. Influence is a form of power, even if we shy away from calling it that. And influencing far less experienced children is hardly the only form of power that adults should enjoy exercising. Kids need to see how they exercise healthy adult power with other adults.

Mission Hill School, like Parker, designed from the start around democratic principles, struggled with how we might engage kids in a recognition of proper adult authority, while also learning how to exert their own powers in useful and effective ways. This required articulating a vision in which young people and adults were equal comembers of a larger community. I learned early on to recognize the need for those rituals of respect for authority that I had at first disdained. While preferring to think that we ruled our classrooms by the authority of our benign intentions and superior skill, helped by the natural desire of the young to either please us or learn from us, we had other powers on our side that needed to be acknowledged. By reason of our age and position we had the power to get kids in trouble, to decide their grades and if they were or were not to be promoted, to reward or shame them in front of their peers, and even to physically restrain them, to mention just a few. What to do about these?

As the letters home that follow suggest, issues of power and authority—whatever labels we used to describe them—came up time after time in the daily tasks of running, or being run by, the community of people who made up our schools. Whether we're talking about school rules, parental voice, decisions about curriculum, discipline or relationships with "downtown," we needed to examine them in light of our respective powers, as well as our respective purposes. Over and over we asked who needs to consult with whom, how do kids' and families' voices fit into the structure of professional decision making, and where do decisions about "policy" end and decisions about "practice" begin. These issues never disappear from the life of the small schools I know best; a few have even reverted to more authoritarian styles as a way to resolve struggles over authority. Most found a balance true to their particulars, one that gave everyone a substantial sense of ownership over the school's "way," thereby creating a strong shared commitment to keeping it afloat as well as opportunities to experience the school as personally nourishing. Smallness was clearly a big part of this—but it is a balance that must be reworked over and over; it always takes fiddling.

And the fiddling can be difficult. Issues of power and authority arouse powerful emotions. Thus, when a kid sent to my office because his teacher has had enough of him then acts sassy to me, I find myself challenged in all the same ways I did thirty years ago as a substitute teacher in Chicago's southside schools. Shouldn't my status as both adult and head of state be enough for this kid? Besides, I like the kid and have some wise and helpful advice for him or her that ought to be listened to. Must I prove myself once again?

It is not so different than when colleagues come to school late, miss deadlines we've all agreed to, or don't let us know when a situation is brewing that is going to blow up in all our faces. Or when colleagues quietly revert to old teacherly habits of privacy or ways in which race, class, and age make people back off from needed confrontations. If I didn't already know how powerless most bosses/principals are at influencing the real heart of teaching and learning, I too might be tempted to revert to a more hierarchical structure.

Teaching is all about bringing kids views out into the open and broadening their vision of possibilities—even about something as "simple" as fractions or capitalization, and surely about something as complicated as power. The great strength of small schools like Mission Hill and Parker is that all these issues of power and authority are addressed, over and over again, in public. Each year the same topics reappear in our letters home. All members of the community are to a considerable degree in on the secret—power is not a dirty word, but something that we are all struggling with using well. We accept the responsibility that comes with our authority, of talking aloud about the when and the how of decision making. We acknowledge the considerable powers the young have—whether we "give it" to them or not—and thus our responsibility to teach them how to practice the best use of their powers. We tell them stories about our own successful and unsuccessful forays with authority—when the policeman pulls us over for speeding, or the superintendent calls us to question something we've done, or when we are in disagreement with each other or our own on-site board.

We like that the size of the school makes it easier to

focus on the topic of authority. The fact that the office is open to both kids and adults means that our phone calls are easily overheard and our many adult conversations are public. This exposure supports our model. At both schools the decisions of those in formal control are, as much as possible, made transparent to ourselves as well as to the kids. When we send kids out for community service or school-to-work experiences, we ask them to look for signs of how authority is exercised there too: who's in charge; how do you know?

Knowing our students over many years makes possible, although not inevitable, that our expertise—the power that comes from our knowledge—can be acknowledged with less unease. At some point, one by one, we notice how kids let down their guard and trust that we have their best interests at heart and that our advice might not be a trick to undermine their own authority. This enables us to encourage students to improve their written work, to look at a math problem in a different way, or to do still another draft. It might even allow us to give them advice about their lives. It seems almost magical when it happens and allows us to spend more time passing on our expertise, less time "motivating" them to go along with us; and from it follows a leap forward in learning. It's true not only with the young—it works amongst the adults in the school too. I tell the kids about how necessary, if galling, it was to do exactly what my teacher told me to when I was learning to fly an airplane—even though he was a third my age and probably no smarter. There was just one thing: he knew how to fly and I didn't. This form of authority can't be taken for granted, as it too often is in schools, families, and workplaces as well.

Getting schools to operate consistent with their own proclaimed goals is a matter of far more importance than most school people acknowledge. It's not just in schools that this issue arises but in the workplaces we are preparing young people for. At our schools it requires our sifting through issues of when to be tough and when not, when we are acting for the child, and when we are protecting the institution, and acknowledging that the two may at times not be the same. We need to recognize that "fairness" and "justice" are complex, that liberty and the good of the community can be at loggerheads. When is it appropriate to act as instruments for other ends (acting on behalf of the larger society, school, or on behalf of a critical subgroup—the handicapped, for example), and when are we there as adults who just plain love and care for our particular charges—no matter what? These are not distinctively "school" issues but are at the heart of the politics of the larger world that our students will influence someday. Thus, how we address them in schools matters not just to "school people" but to the larger society—to lay citizens and not just to educational experts.

# The Letters on Authority from Mission Hill

## BECOMING A PLACE OF RESPECT

*Behind issues of power and authority are issues of mutual respect. What "respect" means—what obligations it imposes, what modes of interaction it demands—feels different when some level of equality can be assumed. Respecting grown-ups and teachers—like respecting the police—in part is just a question of acknowledging the power to coerce. And all schools have some of that, hard as it may be for progressive-minded educators to acknowledge. Then there is also the power appropriately held by people in different roles and with specific expertise. I tell kids about my experiences learning to fly as a reminder about the respect due expertise, even when we are adults. But it's difficult; it's never quite clear to everyone—adults or students—when we mean one kind of respect and when we mean another. This letter was an attempt, once again, to explore these issues.*

Dear Families, Students, Staff, and Friends,

Only two more months and this school year is over! A year ago the Mission Hill School was just an idea, without a home, students, or staff. Now we're a real school. Sometimes I look around and find it hard to believe we've done so much in such a short time.

Being a real school also means facing the messy realities of negotiating different personalities, viewpoints, and experiences. Think of all the complex relationships that make a school: between teachers and parents, teachers and their assistants, students and their teachers, classroom folks and out-of-classroom staff, parents and *other* parents.

Relationships are not developed overnight. They are full of pitfalls. But teaching and learning, it is clear, are at the heart of relationships. We wouldn't have it any other way, even if we could. We tell kids that this means we need to be respectful of each other. Sounds okay, doesn't it? Even obvious.

But kids don't always know what the word "respect" means. As I was trying to explain it to a student the other day, I hit on this idea. Respect is another way of expressing our first "habit of mind." It's about treating others as if you "could be" them. It involves imagining that, in some way, we are all brothers and sisters—enough alike so that we can understand each other if we work at it. It doesn't require approving of or liking each other, but accepting each other's equal "humanness."

Humanness is not always nice, of course. Stepping into others' shoes can be uncomfortable. Can and should we step into the shoes of enemies?

In short, respect is a tough idea. I'm sometimes not respectful because I don't know better—for instance, when I treat others as *I'd* like to be treated but not how *they'd* like to be treated. Treating others as you'd like to be treated is a good first step—but not always enough. Sometimes I don't realize how others hear me. We're using the same words to mean different things. In both cases, being respectful requires me to learn new things. Sometimes we can appear disrespectful because we're thinking about our own interests and blocking out distractions—other people!

Becoming a place of respect will take time. Our staff is visiting sister schools in New York City and western Massachusetts that have been working on it for many years. It's inspiring to see that it can happen. If parents want to be in on such visits, let me know.

The meetings on school norms have been fun. The evening session had almost no parents. But a bunch of kids came by (their parents were at the after-school program meeting) and gave us their thoughts on what they value at Mission Hill, what the rules are, and what counts as respectful. Finding out how the school feels to kids is not easy. Parents, let us know what you learn as you talk about school at home.

—DEBORAH MEIER, *April 13, 1998*

## BEYOND BAKE SALES

*I enjoy telling the story of a very fine teacher and friend whom I overheard saying, as she wearily went home one night, "Next time, I'm taking a job as a teacher in an orphanage." We haven't figured out the issue of working with families, in short. We try a lot of ways, and so do families, and sometimes it still doesn't work. The mistakes we make depend a lot on the balance of power between particular adults, both in reality and perception. These in turn reflect issues of class, race, gender—and probably differ somewhat when parents have the ability to choose schools, as they do at Mission Hill. Clearly, we go back to this over and over because it's central to making schooling work.*

Dear Families, Students, Staff, and Friends,

When you come to see your child's classroom this week, we hope it will make you appreciate your child's hard work and progress and also lead you to ask some complicated questions. Should there be a single definition of what it means to be well educated? Even at Mission Hill? Should families and students help define it by naming their own goals and dreams? How can teachers' and parents' goals be joined on behalf of the children's dreams?

Seymour Sarason, a brilliant school critic, claims there's a natural antagonism between parents and teachers—an equal measure of distrust and misunderstanding. It could be better managed, he thinks, if parents had the chance (and financial support) to spend several days a year full-time in their child's school. An old friend insists that the only cure is meeting with families at least once a month. Everything should give way to such a goal, she insists.

Some argue that only a parent-run school can undercut the distrust; still others say that would work only for those parents who do the running. Some argue we need schools that appeal to particular religious, ethnic, or racial communities—to counter the natural fear that school will undermine the family's beliefs, even unintentionally.

The voucher proponents who want public money for private schools argue that the marketplace is the answer. Let the buyer beware.

Still others think if we prescribe a set curriculum with lengthy, detailed standardized tests, every school will have to do the right thing. Forget the interpersonal stuff, they say. Trust will occur only around objective external measures, with the consequences for failure equally neutral and inescapable.

Some say it has always been thus and always will be thus.

Where do we stand? Mostly we're with Sarason and my old friend: more person-to-person time to work at it together, to see where kids, families, and teachers aren't hearing each other or need more information. Plus some of all the other solutions!

We believe there is a role for parents beyond bake sales—ways to give advice about their own children and a formal voice in making policy decisions. There should be choice—but within the public system. There should be clear standards, without standardization. Finally, we believe some of the tensions may always exist, as we tinker towards utopia.

We want families and teachers to spend more time

together. This week's classroom open houses are a critical part of developing strong family-school collaboration.

Please join us as well at next Monday night's concert and celebration. Creating community is a powerful way to build trust. And music is the magic that often does it.

—DEBORAH MEIER, *December 14, 1998*

## THE RULES: A DELICATE BALANCE

*Mission Hill had only two rules: do nothing that interferes with teaching or learning, and do nothing that hurts or demeans others. But, of course, then come the details. And they are endlessly struggled over. For example, no running in the hall, but skipping is okay. Kids are testing out where we'll pull out our superior rank and fall back on "I said so." And indeed, there is a balance between the school's respect for student opinions and its ultimate authority to set limits, to be obeyed. When the school brings together families with different class, racial, and even religious backgrounds, it can't fall back on implicit assumptions; it needs to be clear and direct. And yet it must also model the importance of due process and the educational value of understanding, not just obeying. How we interpret rights and wrongs is important stuff to get out into the open—it's the central stuff of education. This letter tackles the issue of limit setting.*

Dear Families, Students, Staff, and Friends,

We've been having fruitful, and sometimes heated, staff discussions about "the rules"—that is, what's okay and not okay for kids to do. The list is long, from wearing hats to arguing with adults. It's complicated. For example, we all agree that "bad language" is out, but we don't all agree on what bad language is. Do the circumstances matter?

We make a big point here of encouraging kids (and adults) to ask difficult, probing questions—to look at things from different viewpoints, imagine how others might see it, insist on evidence. Those are our habits of mind.

As we talked, though, we realized that these habits, important as they are, must be balanced by respect for authority and tradition. This discussion was educational for us and could have gone on forever if we didn't have to move on to how to teach reading and math.

We've settled on certain solutions and compromises that cannot possibly please everyone. We'll need to revisit them in time—with students and the Parent Council participating, we hope.

For now, we hope you will back us up on these decisions—even if at times you think we have been too permissive or too strict. A smooth-running, cheerful school is always a balancing act between respecting differences and agreeing to live by some (occasionally arbitrary) rules. Here they are.

*No fighting.* That includes challenges and threats as well as physical acts. We're working out the question of when "play fighting" is truly play and when it's the first step toward a real fight or a cover-up for hurting someone.

*Words do hurt*, so we need to avoid offensive language. There are always other ways to say what needs to be said. Negative references to a person's color, family, gender, racial identity, ethnic background, sexual orientation, or home language are out. So are demeaning references to other people's bodies. By age eight or nine, most kids have a pretty clear idea of what's inappropriate.

Reminder: Certain kinds of body language constitute a physical threat, and certain gestures are a form of bad language. Then there are the simpler no-nos. Do not bring to school anything that might be considered a weapon—including tools with sharp edges. Leave gum and candy in lunchboxes; we don't want them in our halls, classrooms, or play yard. No wearing hats inside the building or coats in class. Clothes should be appropriate for school. Also: no electronic gadgets. If you need to bring them to school, leave them with Marla. Medications must be left with Marla or Christa, the nurse.

Finally, kids need to obey grown-ups' instructions at school, even if we're wrong. There will always be a chance to tell your story and to appeal adults' actions later.

—DEBORAH MEIER, *September 24, 2001*

## HOW WE MAKE DECISIONS

*Mission Hill is governed ultimately by the Boston Public School authorities, though that "ultimate authority" is rarely exercised, except at budget time. At other times, we act as though our Governance Board (made up of equal numbers of parents, staff, and community members, plus two students) were the final authority; and in between their meetings, the Staff Council (which includes the co-principals) conducts the regular life of the school, with input from the Parent Council. It puts decision making close to the action, while also providing for some checks and balances. But in the end, its effectiveness depends on how individual families and individual teachers work out what's best for each child. Because it's "different" we find ourselves often going back and explaining it.*

Dear Families, Students, Staff, and Friends,

At the last Parent Council meeting we talked about the way our school is governed. Our system has two unusual features. The first is what we call "staff governance." Administrators make almost all of the important in-house decisions in most schools. We believe that these decisions should be made, whenever possible, by the people who must implement them. So the adults at Mission Hill—teachers, assistants, specialists, and administrators—meet as a group at least once a week to discuss issues and make most schoolwide decisions. These meetings are open to all.

We arrive at these decisions by consensus—that is, we talk things out until everyone more or less agrees. For legal reasons, the principal retains veto power over decisions that affect kids' health or safety or the school's fiscal integrity. But in thirty-five years of being a principal in staff-governed schools, I have never seen a reason to use this veto power.

At least three times a year the Faculty Council (the head classroom teachers plus the principal, assistant principal, and office manager) meets formally to make basic decisions about pedagogy, curriculum, staffing, scheduling, assessment, and graduation. Teachers take responsibility for implementing some of these decisions, but most of those that relate to out-of-classroom tasks depend on Brian, Marla, and me.

The second unusual feature of our system is our Governance Board. It has sixteen members: five chosen by the Parent Council, five by the Faculty Council, five public members chosen by the board itself, and one eighth-grader, elected by their classmates. Plus alternates for each. The board is co-chaired by the principal and a parent or public member (currently Bruce Smith).

The Governance Board reviews all significant decisions—budgetary, organizational, staffing, and so on—and offers its advice. If there are serious objections, it can send decisions back to the Faculty Council for reconsideration. The board also reviews the principal's annual report. Every three years it formally evaluates the principal and makes a recommendation to the superintendent. (Legally, the Boston Public Schools have ultimate authority.)

It's parents, of course, who know the kids best and have the biggest stake in the school's work. To begin with, they choose the school. Through the Parent Council, they elect parents to the board, share views, give advice, and organize activities. Families also help direct their children's schooling through conferences, as members of graduation committees, and in all the other ways we interact with each other to get the feedback we need to act wisely.

This structure has its plusses and minuses. We think the former far outweigh the latter.

—DEBORAH MEIER, *December 3, 2001*

# The Letters on Authority from Parker

GOVERNANCE

*What goes? What does not go? Who is in charge? Where does power lie? Such questions arise in every school and come from every quarter. Taking a specific issue makes these matters real. "Public displays of affection" was a useful topic for us at the beginning of the school year. It got everyone's attention.*

Dear Parker Families,

One of the tasks during orientation week was a discussion by students and faculty of Parker School "governance." The vehicle for this talk was a case study of where responsibility properly rested for propriety with "public displays of affection," here popularly referred to as PDA. Simply put, who was to decide what sort of loving physical contacts at school were proper and permissible, and why?

Many of you may wonder why we picked this tricky topic as the focus. The matter is freighted with emotions, and for many of us of all ages it is an embarrassing subject. It deals with shifty qualities such as taste, and it borders on sexual issues, topics that many feel should be kept completely private, that inevitably alarm parents, and that both fascinate and frighten adolescents, however cool on the subject they might wish to appear. We chose it both because it is a legitimate issue here at school and because it would get everyone's undivided attention. It was signally effective as a case study of "who decides, and by what right?"

I visited various discussions that were, of course, not so much on "PDA" per se as on who had the right to decide what was proper and how that decision was to carry legitimacy. Thanks to the subject matter, the talk was intense, far more than it might have been, say, on the (also important) matter of grammatical correctness of posters on the walls. It provoked much legitimate First Amendment talk. In a democracy, are there any limits on free expression? Is what might be appropriate out of school somehow inappropriate within school? What of the feelings of those who have to witness PDA as well as those who engage in them? Who has the right to tell one how to feel and how to express those feelings with another person who appears to welcome those attentions?

Inevitably the discussion was self-conscious and, when it came to the question of rules, hilarious. Could a couple hold hands? If so, how many fingers could be entwined? When did a friendly hug become embarrassingly demonstrative, who decided so and by what particulars? Inevitably, to break the tension, someone inquired as to what sorts of PDA Nancy and Ted could mutually enjoy which were denied to those not married to each other. ( I assured them that we were dreadfully shy and old-fashioned.)

Talk of "rules" led most discussions into a cul-de-sac. In one gathering, fortunately, a student made the helpful distinction between "rules" (laws) and "norms" (accepted customs). A norm at Parker might be that each of us would try not to act in any way that was clearly offensive to others. He suggested that to try to define comprehensive rules as to the precise boundaries of "offensiveness" would be onerous, probably even self-defeating. Parker, he argued, should simply be a place where people were sensitive to what others found offensive and acted accordingly.

So easy to say, so hard to do. Most important standards are difficult to set in stone. For example, Thou shalt not lie, ever. But is there no room for what is known as a "white lie," a statement that means only to help? ("That was a great effort . . ." to the shortstop who just committed an error.) Matters of taste present the greatest problems, especially for a crowded, diverse community that runs from an eleven-year-old to a sixty-six-year-old. Thanks to the orientation discussions, most of the Parker community made a fair start at understanding what is involved here.

Within the proposed school governance, any matter

coming before the community for adoption would require a two-thirds majority of "yea" votes both from students and from the faculty, these gathered separately. The straw votes on the PDA issue illumined a generational split: the students would be more generous with PDA than would the faculty. Needless to say, there will be more discussions of all this—PDA and much more of consequence—over the next weeks.

I recount all of this to make a point about Parker. From the very start, we all have wanted this school to be a civil and decent place by reason of the explicit commitment of all members of the community. We believe that the restraint upon which a decent community rests depends on the willingness of each participant to embrace that restraint. We also believe that the hard thinking behind the creation of a civil community is a habit that the students should always carry with them. It's especially important as they enter a culture that today so easily tolerates hypocrisy and dishonesty and which is in so many ways relentlessly tasteless. Parker is itself a world writ small. We should use it to practice what a decent community would be like.

Going to Parker means working hard at these important matters, however embarrassing and confronting some of that work may from time to time be. We made a start last year, with the schoolwide adoption of a Statement of Rights and Responsibilities (a copy of which we enclose in this mailing). This Statement is largely about norms. It was followed this fall by a "contract" (also attached), already signed by 90 percent of the community. We will work at what, as a practical matter, all these norms mean. We will never pretend that such work is easy. The adults will not dodge their responsibilities, and we hope that the students will do likewise.

I hope that families will take the time to talk about these issues—PDA and what it is to be decent and thoughtful—and that your discussions can interweave with ours at school. There is much at stake here.

—TED SIZER, *September 11, 1998*

## LOUD AND SOFT VOICES

*In its fourth year, Parker was a far better school than it had been in the beginning, since it had added consensus and predictability to its creative mix. However, we still faced the challenge of integrating newcomers into our community of "founding" students, parents, faculty and trustees. "The Parker Way," which had been so crucial to us in our initial creation and understanding of our common mission, was interpreted by some as a way to indicate a kind of hierarchy, as in "Let me explain the Parker Way because I understand it and you don't." Students, parents and even some teachers were at times intimidated in that way. This letter was an attempt to endorse the learning that could be gained from other environments than Parker and to include all of our community in our deliberations about the many challenges we still faced.*

Dear Families,

Years ago, when our oldest son was an eighth-grade crossing guard, we had a discussion around the dinner table about a problem he was facing in that work. I remember that I tried very hard not to tell him what to do, but that the next day, his sister accused me of "yelling."

Yelling? I had never raised my voice! Yet she experienced it as yelling, and I think I know why. I was her mother; I was more familiar with the issues than she was; I spoke too fast; and it was clear that I cared a lot.

I am reminded of that experience as I think about the issue of loud and soft voices at Parker. As a noble experiment and a fledgling school, we have special need of loud voices. They are the voices of those who have been willing to take on tremendous responsibility, or who work hard, or who are well spoken or talented in some other way or who know how to connect well with others. In every constituency—teachers, students, and parents—there are people with "loud voices" whom we treasure. Often without raising their voices even the smallest bit, they become important to our community, so that when they speak, they are "loud." They are familiar with the issues and they care a lot.

A democracy that functions properly, however, has to value its soft voices as well. These are the people who are a little less familiar with the issues—usually for understandable reasons, such as being newer to the place—yet who care about our school. They may be hesitant to speak in the faculty meeting, the community meeting or the Parent Forum. They may not be able to get any airtime. They may even feel that the rest of us are "yelling," even shutting them out, when that is the last thing we would want to do.

How should we share the valuable airtime that we have together? Without decreasing or dispiriting our loud voices, how can we listen better to our softer ones? We're going to work very hard this year to find new ways to listen. To do that, we will need to be imaginative about our democracy. Should we design meetings in small groups where more people are likely to speak and be heard? Fishbowl? Jigsaw? Should we write more to each other? Can we find some other approach that we have not thought of yet and have never tried before?

Only the soft voices can determine what will help them to feel more included in our community. We are counting on them to let us know what would help. At the same time, those of us whose voices have been loud will continue to think as hard as we can about this issue and about how we can make progress on it—and on other matters of concern—during this transition year.

—NANCY SIZER, *September 18, 1998*

## DRUGS AND AUTHORITY

*Parker had a "drug problem," both inside and beyond the school. Some students arrived at school acting suspiciously. A few tried to traffic in drugs at or near the school building (or so we suspected). All of this was hard to prove, and many kids were incensed both at our suspiciousness and our invasions of what they considered their private lives. All the parents, not just those of the real or respected violators, needed to be forthright in this conversation.*

Dear Families,

As you may have heard from your children, Nancy and I spoke very directly last Friday to the school about substance abuse in general and illicit drugs in particular. Some possibly troubling disciplinary issues had emerged during the preceding days. We felt the need to be very clear both on our stance on the matter of drug use and on the nest of issues that it provokes.

The easy part is the school's institutional position: any possession, use, sale, or promise to obtain illegal substances will be dealt with sternly. If the law requires, we will seek the assistance of authorities beyond the school. That is Parker's policy. We shall enforce it.

Now the hard part. It is in the nature of growing up to push against authority, that of the school, of parents, and of the community at large. All good schools give students increasing responsibility for their own lives, in essence giving them "learning permits" in many forms. All of us older folk—teachers and parents—know that this is a necessary, healthy part of growing up.

This process is, for parents and teachers alike, a tricky one. The kids push us. We push back. If they push in directions that worry us, we push back vigorously. Often that worry is not justified, and the young people resent our pushing. This is particularly true for teenagers who are attracted to the clothing styles and manner of the entertainment industry's "rebels." When we see them so, we may too quickly conclude that because they adopt the uniform of the drug culture, they must be its prisoner. When the worry is justified, however (whatever the persona adopted by the student), the young wriggle hard to extract themselves (as we adults all too often do in similar situations), lying, shifting blame, attacking motives, ridiculing authority. Inevitably, rumors fly, the tales usually enlarging as they spread. Jokes and idle tales become facts, as incendiary as shouting "fire" in a crowded theater.

We must investigate these rumors carefully—which inevitably draws attention to them—yet in a rumor-filled culture, we must offer each person the fairest possible hearing. Due process is important every where, and especially in a school: the students learn about fairness and the courage of telling the truth by watching us. Neither their task nor ours is easy.

Nancy and I explained all this to the students. Our vocal stand brought reactions. Some students told us that our candor was helpful. Others felt that we had overreacted, that Parker has far less of a "drug problem" than some neighboring schools. If so, we are glad, but any drug problem is a serious problem. We all—school and families—must face frankly issues of this sort, without embarrassment and with the greatest possible care and understanding.

As several students pointed out last Friday, there is much at stake here, indeed the very soul of this school and its community of devoted teachers and wonderfully committed families. Parker must be a decent, safe, and happy place.

—TED SIZER, *October 9, 1998*

## TIME OUT

*Tending the "time-out room," usually our office, was the least fun of being an acting co-principal. I wrote this letter as much to persuade myself that I was not wasting my time as to explain to parents why their Little Darling was cooped up with me for an hour or two.*

Dear Families,

I write this while I supervise Parker's new "time-out" room for some students who have been disruptive in class. Some schools call this routine "in-school suspension." Others have analogous labels. Whatever the name, the exercise is designed to remind students that courteous and careful attention is expected in class as elsewhere in the school. If some do not behave, they come to this "time out," there to work on assignments for the missed class.

I don't like being here. They don't either. But the regimen appears to be necessary sometimes for a few Parker students, at least for the time being.

This kind of activity is usually called "discipline." The word, of course, has several distinct meanings. History is a discipline, a carefully shaped lens on an area of knowledge. In the theater, a disciplined cast of actors overcomes any miscue or unexpected situation; the performers collectively know what they need to do and are responsibly reflective in the doing. Stereotypical old time teachers disciplined their students with smacks of a cane. Fear of such painful and humiliating discipline was to be the engine for an orderly school.

We all want orderly, decent, and safe schools. Equally, we want young people to grow into the habit of disciplining themselves. Self-discipline doesn't just happen: it emerges from practice. Tightly controlled ("disciplined") schools deny such practice and breed angry resentment and contempt. Excessively loose schools provide students who find the game of disrespect more fun than getting on with their work the opportunity to develop selfish habits. All suffer as a result.

Obviously there has to be a middle ground. Parker must have standards. One is that everyone of every age will act respectfully. Another is that there is scope for young people to learn—from examined experience—what respectful action means in practice. It all rests on the idea of reciprocity—I will curb myself now as I know that you might, sometime in the future, do the same for me. Reciprocity implies a common contract, which at Parker is our Statement of Rights and Responsibilities. A commitment to reciprocity grows poorly both in a climate of fear and in a climate of license. And so we end on uneasy, but educationally essential middle ground: punishment that might lead to deeper understanding of what a community rightly expects; and restraint by adults to allow the young room to test themselves in developing a personal code of conduct. Parker must live on this inevitably controversial turf.

Do unto others as you would have them do unto you. Reciprocity. It is simple in the abstract and very difficult in the doing. It is itself a discipline, a lens by which to test the world before engaging in it, a way to act with others in resourceful and principled ways, whatever might be the unexpected interruptions.

I dream about the moment when there will be no need at Parker for "time outs."

—TED SIZER, *March 26, 1999*

## WRITING IT DOWN

*We wanted the respect that adults and students showed each other to come naturally to them, rather than to be enforced. Still, we needed to clarify our expectations, and to do that, we needed to write them down. Three student leaders and I spent the better part of the spring looking up and organizing all the statements about behavior that had been generated by the Community Congress in four years. We wanted to create a student handbook that would support our best instincts and reinforce the tone of decency, which was one of our articles of faith. Of course, the idea that students would write the handbook that would govern their behavior (and that would include state laws, some of which were quite harshly worded) was controversial on all sides. But we made a start.*

Dear Families,

It happens to parents and teachers and advisors and babysitters and employers and leaders of flexclubs and acting co-principals. Someone for whose work or behavior we are responsible is not living up to expectations. What's the best thing to do?

If the co-principal (for example) says nothing, much of the time the problem will take care of itself. The miscreant himself or herself will become aware of changes that need to be made, will resolve to make them and will succeed in making them. That is a win/win, because not only did the co-principal escape the onerous duty of playing the heavy, but also because there is greater learning in something that comes out of one's own perceptions than in something that is imposed by others.

Saying nothing is not a good policy for long, however. Not only is the person in authority beginning to get a little steamed; the wrongdoer begins to conclude that nobody's watching and nobody really cares. The toddler who stands in a puddle waits for his babysitter to protest. The employee whose reports are getting a little sloppy begins to wonder whether it really bothers her employer. The student who regularly blurts out epithets begins to assume that behavior in school is meant to be the same as behavior in the streets. Silence in such a situation is clearly inappropriate. In the absence of words, the wrong conclusions are being made. So we need words, but which words?

The most important words are those that set out the reasonable expectations that we might have of each other. Parker began establishing school and classroom norms and rules soon after the opening of school in the fall of 1995. Considering how collaborative the process was, and how young our students were then, there are some very sensible policies that we established, to which we have added over the years. This year, the Co-Advisors and a leader of the Justice Committee are working to put them in more available written form as part of a student handbook. And every year, within our classrooms and our advisories, students and teachers work to determine what rights and responsibilities they are prepared to assume for the well-being and healthy culture of their environment. Once these expectations are clear, other words—such as those involved in scolding or nagging—become an effective form of communication.

We're good wordsmiths at this school, and our words have helped us to be close to most of our students. In some cases, however, words are not effective; then they need to be followed by punishments such as detention, work duty, suspension or even expulsion. Yet even when a student is being punished, he or she can count on communication—more words—on both sides. As the age range of Parker's students widens, our responses to wrongdoing on the students' part should reflect their ability to learn from others' words and from their own mistakes. The consequences of wrongdoing need to be clear but also appropriate, not only for different violations of the school's rules and norms, but also for the age and experience of the student who has engaged in them. That is the pattern we are determined to achieve.

This year, in a number of different meetings, those of us in every constituency are continuing to think through this complicated problem and sharing our impressions with each other. We are achieving consensus on a number of points. All this takes time and it's a very challenging assignment. We think you would like to know, however, that we believe that we are making progress.

—NANCY SIZER, *May 21, 1999*

# PART III
# Community

# Community

*Deborah Meier*

Children learn about community first within their particular family, and to one degree or another through extended families, geographic neighborhoods, or other affiliations (such as their religious community). For many, school is the first community in which "public" judgments are made about their place, value, and competence by both peers and those in authority. Peer judgments are not always kind, but they are always important; and the objective views of the adults in charge leave long-term marks for good or ill. Workplaces, neighborhoods, and even states and nations are modeled in some ways from our experiences in these earliest communities. Schools today are the central socializers, if not formally then informally, given that so many of us now spend nearly a third of our lives as students in one school or another. This is where we learn how public life is lived, where we fit (or don't) in the pecking order, and how decisions are made, power exerted.

As other institutions—above all, the family and workplace—grow less permanent, schools play an increasingly fundamental role in shaping the meaning of community for nearly all our future citizens. If getting "community" right were at the cost of strong intellectual and craft training, this would pose a dilemma. But it's hardly surprising that this earliest of human endeavors—community making—can be just what's needed for using our hands and minds well too if we do it right.

This is one reason we insisted at Mission Hill and Parker at getting the scale right for a well-designed community. If we need places for children to test out what it means to trust and be trusted, where they can judge the reliability of colleagues, as well as when they must rely on themselves, we need to make it simple enough. We need to play out in myriad little ways the meaning of "my country (family, school, friends) right or wrong" and how we balance loyalty to an institution and loyalty to principles and moral beliefs. We need a place to imagine viewpoints quite different than our own. For this to happen we need to be sure it's a community with differences, as well as one that has ways to expose them respectfully. We need experience with what it means to belong to various overlapping, and even at times conflicting, communities, without being forced to choose. Keeping school means keeping all these issues in mind as they come up around humdrum daily matters, as well as the occasional large-scale ones.

It turns out that community building requires leisure, a fact our students learn about when they study the ancient Greeks, who reserved the vote to those whose occupations allowed for lots of leisure, and for whom the word for school was the same as the word for leisure! The struggle for the forty-hour week was a struggle not just for more comfortable lives but for a more democratic society. Governance requires both knowledge and time. Democratic governance requires it, therefore, for all its citizens.

As we work out all these details we are always engaged in acts of teaching—someone is learning.

Kids are particularly conscious, for example, of the ways schools and families interact and what it means. The school staff and the "home staff" rub uncomfortably up against each other, coming close to blows at times—and even if we try to do it when kids are not around, they "know." In fact, at both Mission Hill and Parker we do most of our interacting right out in the open. Family/school conferences include everyone, reports are all shared, even final Exhibitions are judged by a range of experts, including members of the family. We hold public forums where kids, families, and teachers join together to hear controversial views, and people raise uncomfortable differences. We struggle to keep our means appropriate to the age of the children involved—but we are convinced that on the whole even very young children are intensely aware when tensions are high and that they benefit by not having to guess about the nature of those tensions. We learn to use trained mediators to bring everyone together when ordinary conversation has become unproductive. But we're also aware that some children need more space than others, less intrusion into their private lives; these children thrive on the community as a chance to avoid confrontations. The dividing line between public and private is thin, and it differs for each child and family. One is sure to get it wrong too. Even a child being teased does not always welcome our help. Figuring out how to help the victim in ways that undermine the bully and yet also love both—it's trial and error. But so is it in the society at large. Unintended consequences need to be tracked, since the odds are we'll not get it quite right most of the time. We need a place where we are forgiven. We need to be tough enough while always being mindful that we are not infinitely bendable—we can break.

Each of these dilemmas requires "solutions," which change from year to year. The solutions mean carving out time in the day, week, and year for leisurely conversation; time to observe each other in various settings and to give feedback where we can; time to check things out; time to seek resolution when things get out of hand for any of the parties to the community. This is our form of a judicial system, our legislature.

At Mission Hill we began with the intention of holding five hours of meetings each week, plus twenty professional development days a year to build a collegial professional community. By the second year we added an evening a month for a family school get-together—for food and conversation or show and tell of some sort. Both schools had weekly schoolwide sharing times; Parker had various forms of student and student/faculty governance sessions, judicial courts, and so on. We built rituals that noted both the passing of the school year and the triumphs of the kids—the gateways at Parker, the trimester Exhibitions at Mission Hill, and the super-charged final public Exhibitions upon which the diploma finally rested at both schools. But we also built in rituals that were just "for fun"—trips, hikes, dances, picnics, ballgames. Not surprisingly, food was a big part of all our rituals. Our school walls were full of shared work, and each school built places for both adults and students to chat informally. The offices were designed to feel as though they belonged to everyone, and each school struggled over how to make everything accessible and still protect expensive and fragile machinery!

We had our times of feeling that students were becoming too "familiar"—and our rules too informal; we occasionally called everyone together either to lay down the law or to talk it over together. At Mission Hill, we usually called each other by our first names, and sometimes wished we hadn't. There were tensions between members of the staff—small, short-lived cliques—or longer-lived tensions around race or gender that needed sorting out, bringing into the open. There were disagreements, and decisions had to be made over when to make them public and how to anticipate unproductive fallout.

And then there were questions about who is "us." Who are the "ins," the "sort of ins," and the "outs." Both schools drew their student body from a wide geographic area: Parker from over forty different towns, and Mission Hill from all over Boston. Still, both had immediate communities that needed to be considered. Mission Hill was located in the midst of a fairly tight neighborhood and nearly half its kids lived within a half mile of school. Houses abutted Mission Hill on all sides, and having a good relationship with the immediate neighborhood turned out to be very important—and time consuming. Of course, the larger city of Boston, and state of Massachusetts affected us both. At Mission Hill, the struggles with the Boston Public School authorities were lessons in themselves for our kids, who often heard us arguing with "downtown." In our conversations with the kids in both schools, we talked openly about our differences with the city or state authorities and how we dealt with them—the ways in which we worked to maintain civil relationships if not friendships, tried to understand their concerns, and made compromises where necessary.

The weekly newsletters that went home were one component of this effort to make our work transparent to students, staff, families, and anyone else interested. In part, these newsletters were where we, as acting co-principals, shared our views on what "keeping school" was all about for us and how we thought about our work. But the weekly newsletters were also the way everyone got informed about what was happening schoolwide that week or month; it also provided a lot of details about what was happening within classrooms. A community requires both leisure and commonly shared and trusted information; the newsletters are central to this task. At Mission Hill each classroom teacher also sent home an attached letter each week (these are now incorporated in the schoolwide letter so that everyone can read about everyone!). At Parker the acting co-principal's column was followed by updates on the curriculum in each of the three divisions in each major subject area. Everything was there—too much, no doubt, for many harried families. But year after year, this weekly communication has kept the whole together, and through its pages one can see our ups and downs, our worries and triumphs.

Keeping the school a community—constantly in movement but moving in a shared direction—is not easy, and it takes a lot of support from a lot of different people for it to work. It requires both clear rules and consistencies as well as space for flexibility; it requires lots and lots of patience—alongside dogged perseverance not to let the vision go astray for mere convenience. It works best when we feel we have lots of time, another day to try it out, another year to see it through. A community of this kind, committed to these kinds of values, is what our schools we hope are for many families, children and staff—because that's also the kind of community we want them to seek as members of the larger world outside the school.

# The Letters on Community from Mission Hill

## ON BULLYING AND "TATTLING"

*It was interesting to reread this one five years later. I wrote it in 1998 because we were experiencing a rash of bullying. Now five years later it has emerged as the topic of a lot of soul-searching; we are uncovering a lot more bullying than we were aware of, and not enough "tattling." We had to go back to square one for a while and think about what we were forgetting that had allowed this to become again such a problem. We did a survey and found that nearly half the kids in the school—across all ages—had some experiences with being bullied (and teased) pretty regularly. So, it's not enough to tackle the topic just once or twice. It turns out that it needs to be part of our curriculum and pedagogy on an ongoing basis, as it crops up in every aspect of our work and is a major impediment not only to a civilized setting, but even to learning one's multiplication tables.*

Dear Parents, Students, and Staff,

What students do when they're "on their own"—or mostly so—is very instructive. Beth's weekly commentary, the "News from Outdoors," is a real asset to our work together. It's a delight to discover how many students at MHS enjoy making up their own games and stories at recess, inventing as they go: digging deep holes in the dirt, building "fairy houses," making up plots and dramas.

It reminds me of my own childhood and all our backyard play. It reminds me that we want to be careful about how we redesign our playground next fall. It's fun to see the kids organize and manage their own games and all the new games that come and go. I enjoy watching the mixing of ages and seeing boys and girls side by side. There's more and more of this as the year progresses. Lunchtimes are nicer, too, as there is something almost like dinner-table conversation, at least now and then.

Of course, we don't see everything, and some kids have more trouble at recess than we realize. It may be only a few, but it matters even if it is just one. First, an injury to one is an injury to all. That's an important habit of heart. And second, when we are aware of injustice and don't do anything about it, we lose a little of our humanity. That goes for adults and children.

So all the small forms of bullying that some children experience—and try to make the best of by saying "It doesn't matter," "I don't care," "It's okay, it was just in fun," "I didn't want to play anyway"—are worth attending to. All the children and all the grown-ups need to learn to say: "Hey, stop." Especially the grown-ups, because otherwise kids think it's okay. To witness and ignore is to be a party to injustice. We also need to feel comfortable asking for help when we can't handle it alone. That's not "tattling." It's being protective.

I had one child—out of my three—who spent four or five years as a victim of schoolyard bullying. He outgrew it. That's pretty common. Maybe it even made him more sensitive to others. But it hurt, and I believe it hurt his school and the bullies who did it worse than it hurt him. Our school is very safe for most children most of the time while also providing lots of space for independent and imaginative play. We want to be sure to keep both these qualities and not ever trade off one for the other.

—DEBORAH MEIER, *May 11, 1998*

## DEMOCRACY AND DIFFERENCE

*No community is ever made up of people who think quite alike. But I've always liked best a school community in which the differences help us tackle the broadest social and ethnic diversity facing us. I enjoy it partly because it forces me to imagine how my fellow Americans might be thinking. Thus, the debate the kids had over evolution and the fate in store for non-*

*Christians—a debate that involved us adults as well—was, I thought, invigorating and thought provoking. Also a little dangerous! It made me realize how anxious we get about surfacing our differences. Figuring out how to talk together in ways that allow us to disagree, even fiercely, with each other's ideas without attacking each other personally or impugning each other's motives is tough to do, but it's maybe the most important thing we can teach to youngsters. How else can we hope they will grow up to nourish the democratic experiment? So I cherish the deeply held conflicting views that sometimes surface at Mission Hill, and I also worry whether all of us see how important they are.*

Dear Parents, Students, and Staff,

Lots of the latest school innovations (charter schools, vouchers, choice) sound okay until, as Garrison Keillor puts it, "you stop and think about the idea of the public school as a place where you find out who inhabits this society other than people like you."

Mission Hill is a place where kids meet lots of people who aren't "like them." That's partly what makes working here exciting. Also difficult. Differences can annoy, anger, even frighten us. Parents worry that their children will be exposed to practices and views they disapprove of, challenges to their beliefs. Teachers worry that their comments will be taken out of context, as criticisms of the values of particular families. Kids probably worry too whether it's okay to trust their teachers, and if their teachers trust their families! How far *should* we trust each other? There's no easy answer. We can all agree on our mission statement and yet differ on what it means. It would be a lot easier if we were almost all alike.

But I'm glad we're not. I'm glad we're always going to be struggling to negotiate strongly held differences in a democratic way. I don't mean voting on who's right. In fact, democracy relies mainly on the way we listen to each other before any voting takes place. Can we be open to the possibility that others have something important to say to us, and are we prepared to consider each other's evidence? Democracy also requires that we care enough about each other and the community to give these two habits a chance to work—over time.

I'm reminded of this because of a lively discussion among some of the older students about evolution, creationism, whether human beings were or weren't animals, and other related themes. I was impressed by the kids' capacity to stick to the subject and to present their developing viewpoints. But I also could see how hard it is to accept the idea that someone else sees "truth" differently than we do.

One solution is to avoid the hard issues—politics, religion, sex, lifestyles. But how will we learn to discuss important public questions if we rule them all out of order? And how better to engage children's hearts and minds and develop critical habits than to delve into topics that they have a passion for and opinions about? Some topics really can't be avoided; they are integral to the curriculum. (Besides, in a school like ours where people relate to each other comfortably, it's impossible to stop such discussions from happening.)

Still, we need to strike the right balance. Some habits are more easily developed on issues we don't consider life or death, where we care less. But a central function of such *habits* of mind is precisely our ability to transfer them to other "hotter" topics. Anyone can have good habits when it's comfortable or unimportant. The real trick is to keep those good habits when the going gets rough.

—DEBORAH MEIER, *May 4, 1998*

## ONE FOR ALL, ALL FOR ONE

*To talk about being a responsible citizen seems very hackneyed and preachy. But it goes to the heart of what makes for a good community, which is always fragile and endangered. Putting on a play together and singing together are good metaphors for the value of that "one for all and all for one" slogan that lies at the heart of community. Translating into other domains is always tough going and includes the little stuff (such as picking up litter from the stairwell) to the big stuff (such as speaking up on behalf of a weaker classmate). Sometimes it takes years to realize how much it matters to kids to have been part of, even if for just a few years, a community that lives this slogan. The theme of this letter, written at such a moment was reinforced just a few months later. The reinforcement occurred when former graduates of CPE got together at another reunion shortly after September 11, 2001, in some kind of instinctive gesture to recapture that sense of community at a time when it seemed most fragile.*

Dear Families, Students, Staff, and Friends,

My old school in New York City celebrated the end of its twenty-seventh year and the retirement of its long-time music teacher last week with an evening in honor of the idea "one for all and all for one."

Music is a powerful way of celebrating this idea. It requires the most of each participant, yet the total effect depends on how everyone works together. We each give to all, and in return we all give to each.

Over sixty alumni came, along with many more parents standing in for alumni who couldn't make it. Former students quite naturally took their places alongside the current students to sing their shared repertoire. It was a joining of the littlest to the biggest across several generations, playing music that belonged to them all.

Music was the medium, but the message was far broader. There are many ways of saying it. For example: A chain is only as strong as its weakest link. We remember this not only in music classes but in math, art, and science, on the playing field, and in the hallways. In a quarter century I hope Mission Hill School will be celebrating this message in its own way too.

This idea is central to the mission of our school. We think it helps build academic skills because it provides a setting where it's safe to acknowledge weakness and where there are many motivated teachers of all ages to help us overcome. But it's also a good thing in and of itself.

Schools aren't meant just to sort and select who will be ahead of whom in the climb to personal success.

Inescapably, they do this, of course, and we need to be sure that the playing field is as level as possible in that competition.

But a more important purpose is to help students learn to take responsibility for themselves and their community. Taking responsibility requires being skillful and knowing how to make good judgments. It requires listening to others (like a good musician) and trying to fit in but also knowing when not to fit in—when and how, to stand out.

Taking responsibility in one's community requires knowledge, know-how, and the ability to speak out persuasively. It requires caring enough to persevere even when the going is tough—when it means one more rehearsal, one more revision, one more try, for the sake of everyone who is relying on you to do your best.

Watching us all struggle with this at Mission Hill reminds me how hard it is to do, and also how important it is. Watching the kids in New York City the other night also reminded me how long lasting is the impact of a good school and why it's worth all the effort we put into it—parents, kids, and staff.

We've come far in four years. The evidence is in: this is what counts over the long haul.

—DEBORAH MEIER, *June 4, 2001*

## ALL WORK AND NO PLAY

*Despite a century of rhetoric about play being children's form of work, play is under heavy attack these days. On its way out too is respect for work well done, for good craftsmanship. In a relentlessly labor-intensive society focused on efficient money making, with its narrow definition of productivity, a lot of latent hostility is falling on the young who don't yet feel the rough edges of the external world. The brunt of the attack is falling on play and playfulness, exploration without conscious ends in mind, curiosity for its own sake; the kind of wonder and awe about what we see about us, and why it matters, seem to be idle sidetracks. The children's garden of kindergarten barely exists anymore even for two- and three-year-olds, whom society now watches carefully to see if they can increase their learning curve to ready them for ... life? No—for first grade. It's our conviction that play is important not only for its own sake and for the sake of adult intelligence; it's also at the heart of the kind of leisure that sustains democracy and makes us such relentless nourishers of the arts of playfulness—on the field as well as of the mind.*

Dear Families, Students, Staff, and Friends,

Who gets to play? I don't mean baseball or tennis, but pure play, or playfulness—that is, doing something for its own sake, without any obvious purpose, gain, or goal: "fooling around."

This kind of play is thought to be okay for only two groups of people: very little children and geniuses. But what about all the rest of us? Are we losing touch with the value of play?

When I first began to teach, it was often said that the work of young children was play. That was how they learned to do almost everything and to make sense of the world. They learned to speak by playing with sounds and seeing what happened. When they threw things out of their playpens and high chairs they were playing—and learning from what happened next. When we played peek-a-boo with them they were learning—not just laughing.

We thought a good kindergarten ("child's garden" in German) encouraged this kind of play. The teacher's job was to organize an environment for healthy play. Good play is engaging, provoking, puzzling, and pleasurable.

When I started a school in 1974 in East Harlem, our motto was "Keep play alive as long as you can." We tried to do that, not just through sixth grade, but all the way through high school—with amazing results. Kids of every sort thrived academically.

But today fewer and fewer schools use play to serve learning, even for the wee ones. Lots of teachers and parents seem to feel guilty when they "just play" with their kids. Instead they must "teach." That's too bad. There may be some gain, but the losses are enormous.

We cherish Beth's weekly column because during recess we see play at its purest, and we also see some of the most active learning. I hope you all read it with care. It reminds us that play is not just for certified geniuses.

The courses that our staff and some parents took with Harvard's Eleanor Duckworth during the first two years of Mission Hill (we had to suspend them this year because Eleanor is chair of her department) were often tough, very rewarding, and decidedly playful. Our work at school includes play, we hope: playing with the materials in our classrooms, with ideas at staff meetings, and, of course, with the kids and their ideas.

Americans of all ages work harder today than they did in my youth. In their leisure they try to keep busy or keep entertained. But that isn't play either. It's a serious loss for ourselves and our society when we squeeze play out of our lives. Without it, we're less human, less interesting, and less satisfied people—and probably not as smart.

Even at Mission Hill, we sometimes call the children's play "work," just so we won't feel guilty. We ought to feel more guilty when there isn't enough play.

—DEBORAH MEIER, *November 8, 1999*

## A GROWING FAMILY OF FAMILIES

*We've forgotten an ancient truth: we are who we are because of the company we keep. Creating for our kids an enlarged network of friends and allies is part of our avowed purpose. Thus, our "staff" consists not only of the full-time classroom teachers, with whom kids stay for two years, but of a whole host of other adults with whom kids build relationships over their years in the school. This includes the other teachers, assistants, support staff, the many volunteers who join us for a year or two (or far more), the other families (the parents of their friends and classmates), and the people in the community at whose sides our students often work, whether on a project or in a community service placement. The power of the wisdom informally imparted by this larger network is at least as important as any other lessons we teach.*

Dear Families, Students, Staff, and Friends,

Here we are. It's great to be back together again!

The cast of characters is mostly the same—we have a few new students and families and a few new staff. But the Mission Hill School changes mostly by adding, not taking away.

While our student population has grown from 100 to just 165 over the past four years, the number of adults connected to the school has grown much faster. At our recent staff retreat we realized there are at least ten full-time staff people who aren't part of either house's teaching team. They join twenty teachers and assistants to make for more than thirty adults who are here full-time, plus another fifteen or more part-timers. That's nearly fifty adults in all.

From all fifty of us, to all of you: welcome back to a great new school year.

Who are we? Check out the photo on Page 2 of some of us. How many can you name? We've attached a list of all part- and full-time staff.

Long as it is, this list actually only scratches the surface. There's also our Governance Board, which includes five parents and five community members. And many families come in regularly to help out, speak out, and be heard. They too are an important part of who we are and how this school works. For example:

- Every class needs at least one parent to help out with phone calls, class trips, and by being a representative to the Parent Council;

• The library needs people to shelve books and read to kids;

• We can always use a few extra hands in the lunchroom or the play yard;

• We are always on the lookout for people who can give a few regular hours each week to tutor students one-on-one;

• We need handy and artistic people to tidy up our hall art displays, address envelopes in the office, or run off stuff on the copier. We also need help organizing events: planning and publicizing family nights, book fairs, spring field days, concerts, and so on.

The list is endless.

This school is a community of grown-ups and young people. Children are best raised in the company of many different kinds of adults. We've barely begun to tap the possibilities of what it could mean to our own children, not to mention the larger Boston community, if we really learned to function as a true extended community—a network of networks.

This kind of school culture doesn't happen overnight. It needs continuous nurturing. And it doesn't happen without arguments, differences, and some tears. But it's a powerful part of what gives our kids something special, forever and ever. It's the central idea behind our mission at Mission Hill.

—DEBORAH MEIER, *September 5, 2001*

## HELPING OUR KIDS BLOOM

*Being good kid-watchers is at the heart of being good teachers—and parents. When we fail a kid, it's usually because we weren't watching carefully enough, or sympathetically enough. It's not that kids aren't curious and eager to learn; sometimes we just don't have a clue about what they are trying to make sense of. One of the great advantages of the range of informal contact kids have with interesting adults, and interesting older and younger children, is the oft chance that they will meet a soul mate—if only momentarily—who is trying to make sense of the same thing they are, or who has a special way of revealing a truth, or of connecting to an unasked question. Slowing our pace of life down to where we have a chance to hear each other better is not easy to do. But it's essential and what led to the following piece, written after a week of leisure watching my garden grow.*

Dear Families, Students, Staff, and Friends,

It's great to be back home after several weeks away. The sun is shining, and it's good to get outside and remove the winter debris hiding the tulips, daffodils, and azaleas.

Sometimes school is like a garden. The fruits of long labors appear suddenly and unexpectedly. We wonder when our students will start to bloom. We can't seem to just wait patiently, as we do with plants, even though that might well be the best strategy.

We wonder if we've missed a clue. Patterns emerge that didn't seem to be there before. We notice that one kid always works better when he's with someone who is not a strong authority figure, or with someone who is; when he's working with a friend, or not with a friend; when you offer few choices, if any, or lots of choices; when you make sure there is mostly success, or when you create challenges that are a little out of reach.

We reread Howard Gardner and are reminded that intelligence comes in many forms. We are startled to realize that some kids who have been driving us nuts in class are viewed as productive and smart workers in their Thursday community service placements. All this helps remind us that the kid we see in school is not the whole person.

Some kids are sophisticated readers of books, but not of people—and vice-versa. Given the key role of human relationships in our lives, it's amazing how little attention we give it as a form of intelligence. But schools like ours take it seriously. That's why we spend so much time talking with and just being with kids, formally and informally.

It's also why we organize the school so that kids see us interact with other adults—colleagues, families, visitors. But just showing them isn't enough. We need to help kids decipher, decode, translate these experiences, for experience can misteach as well as teach.

A recent study found that adolescents spend only about 5 percent of their waking hours in interactions with their parents. They spend nearly a third totally alone, a third with peers, and a third in school—mostly in schools where they do not have close relationships with adults. That's scary.

As I walk around this place, I'm struck by how much of our school third is taken up with adult-student conversation. And we're planning new after-school clubs and study halls for next year to strengthen those relationships.

We also hope that you sit down at home and figure out whether you are among the families who have gotten too busy for the leisurely conversation and play that kids need to have with adults who know them and care for them. This kind of homework is essential—not just schoolwork, but true home-based work, the passing on of your wisdom to your own kids. It can't be done in a hurry.

—DEBORAH MEIER, *May 8, 2000*

# The Letters on Community from Parker

## PERSONAL LEARNING PLANS

*At Parker, all students devise their own "personal learning plans" each year. Much of the advisors' counsel of their ten to twelve advisees involves helping them to set realistic but challenging goals and then identifying the strategies that are most likely to help them achieve those goals. Goals may be as literal as achieving a gateway in a certain subject by midyear or the end of the year; they may be as general as reading more books or being less impatient with a younger brother. The goals are revisited all year, and by year's end, a student's progress is often expressed in terms of his own goals. As a process, it will probably never be simple or easy. But writing down their own goals and subjecting them to the scrutiny of their advisor, teachers, and parents has proven to be an effective reminder to the students that their own accomplishments are what school is about.*

Dear Families,

In many respects, Wednesday was an unusual day at Parker. Instead of meeting in classes, it was characterized by conversations between a small number of individuals who are important to each other. Instead of a fascination with the present—which always seems to prevail in any atmosphere largely peopled by adolescents—there was an intense interest in the future. What would Parker students choose to make their most important educational goals for this year? And what strategies would they choose to help to carry them out?

For weeks, the Parker teachers have been like squirrels, gathering pieces of paper and putting information on the common computer in the faculty room to ready themselves for Personal Learning Plan Day. During a workshop for new advisors on what to expect, Ted and I even took part in a role-play—we were parents, with Jodi as our child and a somewhat flustered Matt as the teacher trying to deal with us. Advisories have been devoted to helping students address these large questions, and parents have been asked to come to school prepared to have these important discussions.

When the 28th finally came, we felt ready. In every corner of these two floors, there were little clusters of people carefully considering words. We do that every day, but this day was different, because the words had been chosen for their specific meaning and for the power they might have to focus our work and to give us energy.

"This is so much better than report cards," one mother who is new to Parker reported enthusiastically. "It's two way," she continued as her daughter stood next to her smiling but also rolling her eyes. "It's a conversation, not a report."

And, of course, that is the point. A conversation gives us all a chance to follow up on each other's ideas. It is not a vague, all-purpose statement susceptible to "spin." Parents and teachers have each taken a day out of very busy work lives to concentrate on the purposes and the practices of the student whom they have in common. They are not discussing the student behind his or her back, however. The student, uncomfortable as she may feel at first, is the most important member of the trialogue. No matter how much we all help, she is the only one who can make the personal learning plan work.

It was a long and exhausting day for the teachers, but one that, in our experience, turns out to be worth it in nearly every instance. Even the difficult conversations are illuminating. If the goals set are truly close to the students' hearts and if the strategies turn out to be wisely picked—or wisely altered as circumstances dictate—that day will turn out to be the most important one of the year.

—NANCY SIZER, *October 30, 1998*

## SPENDING TIME TOGETHER

*Our school started with 120 twelve- and thirteen-year-olds whose parents, living in different towns over a wide geographic area, came to know each other in the process of creating our school. Four years later, with a larger and inevitably less tight parent community, our parents needed to know and to trust each other in a variety of new ways, mostly concerning the social lives of their children. "Everybody does it" feels even more menacing to an anxious parent when "everybody" lives so far away. Perhaps because of our start-up status, we had a large proportion of eldest children in our student body, with the inevitable education that all of us need when our children are not quite adults. Smaller meetings with the "advisory" mothers while we planned these larger Parent Forums on "growing-up issues" were revealing and heartfelt. The topics, chosen by parents and teachers, were tackled with both information and discussion.*

Dear Families,

"My candy days are pretty much over," one Parker student explained to another just outside our office door, shortly after Halloween. I have no idea what led to that remark, but I can guess what it signifies. Our students are growing up, and they know it. Most of them are sensible about it. A number of them are taller than we are now, and their cars are taking up more of the parking lot. These are just the outward signs of a change that is even more tremendous within each one of them. What can we do to adjust to this change? What can we do to help?

Since they are growing up, every year our students are spending a greater proportion of their out-of-school time together. Most of the get-togethers that the students organize are very successful from everyone's point of view, and their desire to spend time together is a sign of our success in creating a community here in Building 2602.

Yet it's also disquieting. This is a fascinating and impressive age group, but it is also one that has a different sense of risk than we do. Parents of teenagers all over the world are being asked to react to the following questions: "How come you're the only one who has a problem with our plans?" "It's my homework! Why do you care?" and the old favorite, "Don't you trust me?" These questions are never easy to answer. Parker parents, however, face an unusual situation. We are spread across more than thirty towns, and we therefore do not know each other as well as we wish we did. It's hard to approve of plans when you can't put a face on the friend mentioned, let alone his parents. The distances seem vast, the drivers inexperienced, figuratively and even literally.

We are planning two events for Tuesday, December 1, to talk with each other about all this. The Health Advisory Council invites all parents to join them at 6 p.m. to discuss the question of "Where are the patterns in our relationships?" in order to shape our sexuality education curriculum. At 7 p.m., the Parent Forum will focus on the growing-up issues that have been identified as most important by both parents and teachers. We hope that a large majority of our parents will join us for what we are sure will be an important event.

As one parent said, quoting the African proverb, "It takes a village to raise a child." Their "candy days" may be over, and our children may not be "children" any longer. But if we know each other better, we can be a more supportive village.

—NANCY SIZER, *November 24, 1998*

## HAVING A LIFE

*Between Thanksgiving and the winter vacation, the personal lives of our teachers became more apparent: they were planning trips, assembling gifts, organizing parties. At the same time, the professional demands on them showed no signs of easing up. In fact, vacation itself created a sort of stress for some of our students, who then turned to us for help with it. And projects needed to be finished up, assessments provided, decisions made about midyear curriculum. Juggling several different kinds of work at this time of year is not unique to Parker; all good schools have a version of it. Still, it seemed like a good time to remind ourselves and each other that even in a school noted for how hard its teachers work, it is still a good idea to "have a 'life.'"*

Dear Families,

"Does anybody out there still do windows?" is the ad that I'm considering running in our local newspaper. "Public school acting principals too busy doing civic duty to take care of things at home."

Recently, a Parker parent asked us how we were "holding up." The fact is that we are having a great time and appreciate Parker more than ever. We may look pretty tired some days, but we will not, we assured her, wear out before our term is over.

Still, "taking care of things at home" is on the minds of all of us who work at Parker, especially during this season. I have a theory as to why this may be an even greater challenge for us than for many other workers. Parker people, you will agree, are unusually willing and skillful nurturers. The very qualities that make them interested in your children also make them important to their own—and to their parents and grandparents and friends and neighbors. They are the parent whom a child calls when he is upset, the daughter who can help her mother through an illness, the grandson who calls to find out "how everyone is doing."

Dirty windows are easy, because they can be postponed. Toothaches and heartaches—their own and others'—are harder to manage. At times their children and their parents need them exactly when their students need them too. Should she wrap presents this weekend in order to send them off on time, or should she assess those papers? Should he stay at this meeting, or should he drive his daughter to her lesson? Should she stay to help one more student, or should she get home when she said she would? And what plans should we make for the summer?

Don't get me wrong. I really believe that, most of the time, jobs and family life complement each other nicely. Our own grown-up kids were quite wary at first about our decision to offer to do this job. Evidently they exchanged quite a number of e-mails about it, blaming the daughter who lives nearest to us for "letting" us "do such a *crazy* thing." Recently, however, one of our sons wrote us that he was withdrawing his objection. "Sitting on the porch a couple of weeks back, you both seemed so engaged, thoughtful, and happy." He likes what the job is doing for us. And if we can play a small part in making our public school successful, we believe that we will somehow help his children's school too. Doing our civic duty is also taking care of things at home.

Besides—I might as well confess it—our windows never were that sparkling, even when we had more time.

—NANCY SIZER, *December 11, 1998*

## STUDENT LEADERSHIP AND CELEBRATION

*At Parker, we had a Constitutional Assembly in the first year, in which students played a vital part. We then had a Judicial Committee, and the equivalent of a house of representatives, with students elected by their advisories and teachers by their colleagues. The "senators" were our idea, as short-lived in Parker governance as we suspected they would be, but helpful indeed. "Senators" were the older students who had experienced some of the frustrations of politics but who still had a desire to help the school to succeed. They had the ability too. The tone they set, the responsibility they took, the way they performed both before and during our inspection was one of the high points of the year.*

Dear Families,

I know from raising my own kids that a parent always likes to hear when someone has enjoyed being in his or her child's company. Let me tell you about two times during this lively pre-vacation winter week when I really enjoyed the kids at Parker.

The first was in our dealings with the "senators."

These, in Sizer-speak, are the "older, wiser" students who are interested in being leaders of the school. The whole concept is flagrantly unconstitutional by Parker standards, but the students are humoring us since we are here for only one year and since they are self-selected. We met once last spring, and they were the students who came often during the summer to help us to create the decision-making model that has since been adopted by the Community Congress. Many of them are also the leaders of the flexclubs, and a few are in the Community Congress and the Justice Committee. Like older students in every school, they are cultural leaders as well.

We called the "senators" back because there was an important job to do. About thirty students met with us twice to learn about the inspection, which will be part of our charter renewal, and on Tuesday morning during an extended check-in, they each described the inspection to a different advisory in the school. As I walked around the school that morning, I heard them explaining why the inspection is necessary, what a "shadow" is, and what will be required of all of the students during those three days. From what I could tell, they also answered questions well. In our meetings with them that morning, I could sense their good will, their desire to help their young school live up to its best version of itself. And in large part because of our emphasis on oral presentation, they were skillful at meeting what for some high-school students would be an impossible challenge.

The second happy event for me was when we all trekked down to the sports arena to take part in a gateway celebration. This event was changed somewhat this year, since the midyear numbers have grown so much that we wanted the whole school to take part. Parker is about progress, both academic and social. It is about more than the individual. We achieve this progress more by collaborating with each other than by competing with each other. In the faces of the students that afternoon was the ability to glory in each other's accomplishments and to realize that each of us is enhanced when another is honored.

Clustered in the bleachers on one side of the hall, the students were rowdy in a good cause. They cheered as the gatewayers went up to the front to receive certificates from their teachers and flowers from their advisors. The respect between teachers and students was also evident in the numerous handshakes and hugs that were exchanged. After the ceremony, those of us who had not done a gateway this particular time made an arch through which the gatewayers passed with a combination of embarrassment and pride. We all then enjoyed some parent-provided refreshments and walked back to Building 2602 in happy groups. Having the celebration in the afternoon rather than the morning might have lost some parents, though you were all invited, and it was an event that I believe any parent would enjoy. I talked with one parent later, however, who told me that she felt that her son's actual gateway was extremely "parent-friendly," so it felt fine to her that the celebration this midyear was with the largest possible number of his student and faculty friends.

What a group! They're all yours next week, but, believe it or not, I'll miss them.

—NANCY SIZER, *February 12, 1999*

## WRESTLING WITH OUR DREAMS

*Reformers for centuries have been tempted to promise too much. Changing anything is inherently difficult, and to get up enough energy to take risks and to do that much work, one has to imagine a new and much better outcome, almost a utopia. And then—surprise, surprise—you are trudging toward this ideal with mere mortals on either side of you. In fact, you are a mere mortal too! While some of us were terrified of "mission drift," I found myself equally impatient with those whom I privately called "purists." As an articulate and reflective bunch of people, we managed to worry about all of it. At the same time, school kept, the kids did well, and more and more applied to join our lottery.*

Dear Families,

Rob Evans, the author of a book called *The Human Side of School Change,* told the faculty this week about a school that gives an award, every faculty meeting, to that member of the faculty who is brave enough to describe a project that was well planned and earnestly carried out but was nevertheless a disaster. Admitting such mistakes brings perspective to a community and elicits the kind of humor that we need as mere mortals to try to adjust our practice to our ideals. Ever since I have been involved in Parker, one of its delights for me has been its ideals, and its promise. Imagine a group of colleagues who are all drawn to a school because of its progressive nature. Imagine a group of students who are willing to leave the familiar and take the risk of participating in a new and better kind of education. Imagine a group of parents who are willing to drive their kids to school, and then stay to help it. Imagine a curriculum that is designed with student engagement as its highest priority, its surest route to real understanding. And, for Ted and me, imagine that the people behind all this benevolent and purposeful activity are open and even welcoming to a couple of old-timers who still find schools the most fascinating of all the places they could be.

Imagine all this, and dream, and then work to make it so. We have all—trustees, teachers, students, parents—been dreamers. With dreams, however, come grandiose expectations. Why can't we have every possible part of the curriculum perfectly taught, every desirable service offered, every student responsible and respectful, every teacher in a perpetual state of preparedness and good humor, every parent a full partner in our mutual job of raising their young? Why isn't every class for every kid a wonder, an inspiration, a definable step forward? Why have we all, after nearly four years, still got so much left to do, and when we haven't done it—or even can't do it—why do we feel so guilty?

At times, the perfect can become the enemy of the

good. "Vision" still sounds okay to me, and "goal" seems fine, but I've grown wary of the word "dream." If I don't reach my goal, I will feel that tomorrow is another day, and I can chip away at more of it then. There is a sense of accomplishment. Dreams, however, are all-or-nothing, and by morning, they are gone. Vaguely remembered, they can leave behind a faint sense of having lost something. They can haunt us with the sense of compromising our original mission and keep us from developing new and realizable goals as we move into a new era. If our only ideal is perfection, we can be too hard on ourselves in the middle of this vibrant and heartwarming place.

Good progress is being made nearly every day here at Parker: by students, by adults, for our school as a whole. We aren't perfect, but we're still all remarkable people who frequently take joy at doing our best in the many things we do and still have left to do. Toward the end of our fourth year, we need to celebrate ourselves and the fact that we are beyond mere promises and moving sturdily toward so many of our wonderfully worthy goals.

—NANCY SIZER, *April 16, 1999*

## WHAT IS PARKER?

*Restating our raison d'être—exactly who we at Parker were—was timely, given the state inspection just behind us and a new principal shortly to be appointed. Putting such words down and sharing them is a useful reminder at any and every time.*

Dear Families,

What is Parker? Across our community and beyond, images inevitably pop up, several in the last fortnight.

Some images are almost meaningless in their generality. Parker is progressive. No word in American education these days has more, and often conflicting, definitions. Some images stray from reality. Parker only wants students who score well on standardized tests so that the school will look good. Absolutely false. Parker is a rich school, spending more per pupil than comparable secondary schools in the region. False again. Parker is not a public school, accountable to elected authorities. Wrong again. Parker decides which students come and which do not. Wrong yet again.

So what is Parker? It is a secondary school that is inventing itself. It is not the expression of some Model Delivered from on High, "put into place," as much current education jargon would have it. The common principles of the Coalition of Essential Schools provide a base, but the practical expression of those ideas arises from an often cumbersome process that involves trustees, teachers, students, and families. Every year this expression has been adjusted, both because the school is growing and because we did not get it quite right the first time. The ambiguity inherent in this process is awkward, but it is the necessary price of having a place that secures its legitimacy by engaging everyone in its creation and evolution.

So what is Parker for this acting co-principal? It is a truly public school, a place that admits families by lottery without regard to where they live, whether in "expensive" or "less expensive" towns and small cities. It is a place committed to helping each young person use his or her mind well; we accept the reality that without intellectual confidence and competence, a person cannot survive in modern society. If we appear to push hard on that dimension, so be it; but let it be remembered that this school is committed to every child, without exception.

Parker is a place that accepts the reality that no two of us—young person or older person—is quite the same and that to the fullest possible extent we will simplify our program to make it possible for each teacher to know his or her students well. The school will try to adapt its work as immediate conditions require. All this is not easy: Parker is an underfinanced school, given the manner in which charter schools have been funded by the state legislature.

However, creating a school like this is a goal worth pursuing. The costs burdening the familiar, large anonymous high schools in the country are all too evident. The risks we are taking are worthy ones.

—TED SIZER, *April 30, 1999*

## TWINS AND DIFFERENCE

*Reinforcing Parker's commitment to "know each child well" was easy to write for a grandfather contemplating his daughter's newly born twins. Such a letter was possible in a small school; some parents and most of the students and faculty mem-*

*bers had met the new mother and father; all knew us well enough by then to see Nancy and me as parents too. Parker was a community, and acted as such, and this in the shadow of the Columbine tragedy that had happened but weeks earlier.*

Dear Families,

Those of you who have been at school this week may have noticed Nancy's absence. She has spent the last ten days in Bronxville, New York, helping our daughter Lyde and son-in-law Jim Cullen with their newly born twin boys and five-year-old son. Some Division III and Division II students may remember Lyde and Jim; Lyde, who teaches at Sarah Lawrence, and Jim, who teaches at Harvard, talked recently at Parker about what it means and what it takes to be a successful first-year college student. The suddenly larger Cullen family is doing well, and the twins are flourishing during their first fortnight of life. We are grateful.

This is our family's second set of twins. In both cases, Nancy and I have been powerfully reminded of the commonplace that each child born into this world is profoundly unique. The same gene pool, yes. The same hour of birth, yes. The same early nurturing, yes. But through it all, even in the earliest days of life, there is emerging distinctiveness. It is a bland truism that each of us ultimately is but ourselves (even among identical multiple siblings); but at the same time, especially when one confronts this miracle in one's own immediate family, one never fails to marvel at this mystery.

How unfortunate it is, then, when we try to package

young people as they grow older, to expect them to be in the same mold just because they are the same age, or same gender, or same race, or same shape. Tragedies such as that at Columbine High School terrifyingly remind us of differences; yet, in the torrent of ink since that horror, the stereotyping continues. "American adolescents will . . ." Somehow the gentle specialness of each child, smothered by harsh talk of the "specialness" of two apparent assassins, gets lost.

At a recent faculty meeting, each of us was offered the chance to record that which was "most essential" for us as Parker teachers, and thus most precious to guard as we made budget and program decisions for next year. Above all, what emerged was the need for each of us "to know our students well." How can one teach well if one does not know each child well, even if two of those children happen to be, like the newcomers to our family, twins? Each is distinct, her or his own person. Worthy schools respect that in their design, in their student-to-teacher ratios. We at Parker must always treasure it.

—TED SIZER, *May 14, 1999*

# PART IV
# Standards

# Standards

*Theodore R. Sizer*

"Standards" has become the trumpet call for American school reform during the last two decades. The word is unassailable: Who can be against standards—that is, high standards? And who can credibly argue that the majority of American schools are functioning at a high standard and thereby graduating students who meet a high educational standard?

The rub comes with what precisely is meant by standards. Who exactly has the authority in a confident democracy to set and monitor them in a way that is respectful of and not intrusive to serious teaching? The rub becomes especially abrasive when the word is used by state (and now federal) government as a weapon and as a condescending pejorative: "You have low standards and, because we no longer trust you, we must move in on you and raise them." Our two mid-1990s, early-2000s schools worked and continue to work within such a condemnatory political climate.

The currently titled "standards movement" has two, often unconnected, strands. The first has to do with subject matter. What facts, skills, and attitudes, for example, represent "high-standard senior high school United States history"? What are the areas, skills, and operations that should constitute eighth grade mathematics? What are the essential "reading skills" for fourth graders? As in most states, Massachusetts leaders appointed committees to answer these questions, and a string of "curriculum frameworks" emerged. Predictably, these frameworks were a varied lot, some persuasive and imaginative, some wooden, some demonstrably wrong headed, some suspiciously ideological. For understandable political reasons (all sorts of interest groups want their piece of the action), most frameworks cover more ground than most experienced teachers think wise. Coverage inevitably trumps depth, and, with it for many students (many teachers believe), deep and sustainable understanding.

The second strand has to do with assessment. Describing the domains to be studied was one thing; ascertaining that such study was—student by student—accomplished was another, and far more difficult, matter.

Not surprisingly, testing has become the lightning rod of the standards movement. Many citizens and teachers in most states have come to believe, as we do, that on the whole the tests are ill designed, misleadingly scored, and a diversion from serious learning.

Standardized tests necessarily tend to break up knowledge and understandings into small pieces ("items," they are often called) or simplistic patterns ("the five-paragraph essay," scored on the basis of a rigid formula). Tests stiffly assess the here and now, the recent "coverage" of "material." Education, however, is ultimately about habits, what our young people think and do beyond school, when no one is looking. What those young citizens learn in school is a means to that end, not an end in itself. A score on a well-designed standardized test can tell us something about a student but hardly everything, and rarely about habits (save the persistence required to endure long, quiet hours in a test room).

Neither of our schools ignored standards or the expectation of frequent and demanding assessment. But from our beginnings we posited what we feel is a deeper, more authentic, and more sustainable system of multiple, indeed daily, assessments using the students' work (ultimately assembled in portfolios). These actual physical collections of work display progress (or the lack of it) over time as well as various kinds of exercises, from public presentations to standardized tests, including the Massachusetts Comprehensive Assessment System (MCAS). The standards at which these collected data aim are carefully and publicly described and expressed. At both schools, for example, they appear as charts on classroom walls and within personal learning plans that are discussed regularly with the student, several of his teachers, and his or her parents or guardian. Both schools urge—indeed, require—family engagement with the specific academic work of its child: Every student (not only those with "special needs") has a personal learning plan. Both schools assume that a child learns best when teachers and family members are as one on the specific tasks and hurdles facing that child. It is out of such a comprehensive focus that intellectual and social habits are most likely to emerge.

While the detailed standards outlined at both schools are rarely at irreconcilable odds with those imposed by the state, they go further and deeper, and the students (particularly the older ones) understand the reasons for them and the level of performance required. In this way, standards are part and parcel of every day's work, not something foreign, cramped by the technology of a single assessing device, and imposed by distant authorities *ex cathedra*.

The gap between state regulation and the committed practice of our schools has caused awkwardness. We public school principals are at once officers of the state and shepherds of our particular schools. The demands of the first sometimes clash with our duties as the second. All of us, especially Deborah, have written about this matter in other books, challenging the status quo and highlighting the inconsistency between our informed beliefs and what we as public servants insist upon. Some of the letters that follow reflect both the ambivalence that we feel and our need as school leaders to inform our families of the issues involved.

However, we are happy to report that imbedded in Massachusetts charter school regulation is an alternative to the crude testing and ranking represented by the MCAS standardized testing: the "inspection." During our year as Parker's acting co-principals, state inspectors spent most of a week at the school, considering evidence that we were true to our charter, including its academic and personal standards. The inspectors looked at all sorts of student work, visited classes, and studied independent evidence, including scores arising from MCAS and Stanford 9 tests. They saw not just a narrow, indisputably distorted snapshot of our school but a fair slice of its work in progress. That the state countenances and depends on such inspection suggests that a better of way of oversight in the name of "standards for all schools" is not politically out of reach.

# The Letters on Standards from Mission Hill

PARENTS' AND TEACHERS' ACCOUNTABILITY

*One of my gurus, Seymour Sarason, argues that if we could get the parent/teacher relationship right, everything else would pale in comparison. If we had it right, probably the big brouhaha about "accountability" would have had a harder time gathering steam. But trying to take apart what we mean by "being accountable" is absolutely essential. This was one attempt I made, starting by going back to my role as a parent and ending up with what works for us at Mission Hill. We try a million ways, but we're still just scratching the surface. If we had time for a lot more face-to-face, would this work better?*

Dear Families, Students, Staff, and Friends,

With all the talk about accountability and assessment, I've been thinking about how we, as parents, are "accountable" for our parenting, and how we assess how well we're doing. It was hard. Some nights I would fall asleep thinking I'd been a complete failure as a parent. Other nights I felt pretty confident that I was on the right track. And then all those in-betweens.

Sometimes I tried to think "systematically" about my kids. I divided my evaluation into three areas: How they dealt with their family, with their friends, and with schoolwork.

One of my children got along fine with his peers but didn't have close friends. Another had a few dear friends but was otherwise sort of a loner, not part of a group. Should I worry? One child read at every chance she could get (including times I wanted her to be doing other things), and another rarely chose to read for pleasure. But what he chose to do instead was always interesting. Should I worry?

One child was especially generous, another musically talented, and another helped organize us all. No one obliges us as parents to rank or compare our children. And no one is looking over our shoulder to make sure our evaluation of them is fair or statistically reliable. We just try to make sense of our children and to help them.

I imagine that home-schoolers think this way. Once in a while they may give their kids a task that allows them to make comparisons with other kids. But most of the time the kids are judged by someone who is just trying to get a good picture and to figure out what might be the best next step.

I hope that's what happens here at Mission Hill too.

But we have a more complicated task. As parents we feel accountable to ourselves. But as teachers we are accountable to parents, at the very least, so we try to imagine what they need to know and how our view matches theirs. At Mission Hill we're also accountable to our colleagues, so we need to share our evaluations in ways that help us all get better at what we do. Of course, we're also accountable to the people who pay us and want to know if we're doing a good job.

It's not easy to figure out one evaluation method that satisfies these different purposes. As you get the short reports we have just sent home, give us feedback. Are they worth the long hours spent writing them? How do they compare to one-on-one conferences? How about the time spent on weekly teacher letters? Does homework help you know your child's work ways better?

We shouldn't spend all our energy on what's wrong with the MCAS. More important is to figure out what works for us—as parents and teachers and a school—to know ourselves and our kids in useful ways.

—DEBORAH MEIER, *January 24, 2000*

## STANDARDS YES, STANDARDIZATION NO

*This was an early effort on my part to connect the issue of schooling and trust. The five things I laid down are probably as true today as they ever were. The fourth one—public resources—is taking a tough whacking right now, while the second—testing—is far worse than I imagined in 1999. But, at least at Mission Hill, the first, third, and fifth are doing well.*

Dear Families, Students, Staff, and Friends,

The following is adapted from an op-ed column I wrote for the Rochester (N.Y.) *Democrat Chronicle.*

After thirty years as a so-called school reformer, I'm finding myself at odds with a lot of what's now called reform. The schools I've led have been much touted for their extraordinary success with ordinary children. We learned, above all, that even our best ideas wouldn't work if imposed on the unwilling.

This is not a time to give up on the historic American idea that The People can be trusted—in the long run. *Trust leads to trustworthiness, and the reverse is equally true*—with kids and grown-ups. Respect for teachers and families are two ideas we should not abandon, and nothing suggests we need to. Where American education does look bad is only in the gap between our top and bottom students. But then we look far worse than any other industrialized nation if we compare income, health care, or money spent per child between the top and bottom. These inequities are a national shame. Some can be helped by good education; some can't.

What's most needed? First, more contact between grown-ups and kids. Education is largely about the company we keep. We need more adults keeping company with kids. We need smaller schools and smaller classes. Community service programs are another good way to increase contact between kids and grown-ups. Too many adults don't know our kids and their schools, and too many kids, especially adolescents, don't know many grown-ups or their worlds. We're living dangerously separate lives.

Second, we need to end the mandatory testing frenzy. Let's stop pretending we can make high-stakes decisions affecting individual children (promotion, graduation, etc.) based on a single test designed by distant experts with questionable agendas. Local communities should have the authority to give whatever tests they think will help *them.* State mandates should not overrule local decisions about how best to assess their schools and children. Standards yes, standardization no. There should be plenty of public review but far less public mandating.

Third, we need choice in public education: sufficient *public* choices so that few parents will feel the need to opt out—except when they want things our Constitution says they can't have at public expense (e.g., an all-white school).

Fourth, we need sufficient resources so that poor and rich start on a more nearly level playing field—before, during, and after school hours. Do they go to school in buildings with similar facilities? Are their teachers equally well prepared? Again, the gap between top and bottom is a national embarrassment.

Finally, young people must be surrounded by grown-ups who are in the habit of exercising good judgment—who rarely have to say, "Who, me? I'm just doing what I was told to do."

—DEBORAH MEIER, *June 1, 1999*

## THE MOST IMPORTANT REPORT

*The point of this letter was as much to remind my colleagues why this annual narrative report was critical as it was to remind parents. Still, it's the hardest form of work we do, and it's very time-consuming. We're still struggling over it—how to hit it right, whether these need to be done yearly, and whether they should come before or after family conferences, which take place twice a year. When we get it right, it's probably at least as useful to us as to the family or student. But that doesn't happen every time.*

Dear Families, Students, Staff, and Friends,

Our students spend just about a fifth of their waking hours with us at school. In a way, that's not a lot of time. But we see a side of them that families don't—just as you see a side that we don't. This spring's narrative report is our chance to share what we see.

Twice a year—at midterm and again at the end of the year—we give you a report in which we try to cover mostly the academic side of things. In those reports we hope to give a clear picture of progress made in different areas as well as some comparative information. That's what those checks and check-plusses and brief comments are about—for example, "Good progress in X, but still not at grade level." Getting those two reports clear is hard work, and the feedback we've gotten suggests we're closer to the goal this year.

Twice a year we have formal family conferences to look at the student's actual work and discuss it.

In between these times we gather all kinds of information—some on a daily basis and some at special, more formal moments—to share with you. For example, twice a year we tape-record children reading and score their performance—until they are fairly fluent. With older fluent readers we conduct a formal reading survey and interview at least once a year.

We collect writing samples to score at least twice a year—once scored by the classroom teacher and once by two other readers. We are now formally assessing kids at least twice a year in math using several measures, including a locally developed Boston Public Schools test that follows the investigations curriculum that we use at Mission Hill.

Then there are our time-consuming seventh- and eighth-grade portfolio reviews. And, of course, the Stanford 9 and MCAS standardized tests, if you request them.

Perhaps the most important report for us, though, is the once-a-year spring narrative. In it, we try to describe as fully as we can (within a few pages) how your child works at school, how she spends her time, what he is most interested in, how she makes friends and relates to adults—in short, what he or she looks like to us. That's the one that we've been working on for the past month.

Writing twenty of these reports is tough work. It requires careful marshaling of evidence, lots of reflection, and more skill as writers than we necessarily have. It's hard to put such stuff down on paper. We work on these individually, in small teams, and with partners, in an effort to get them just right. But of course we don't ever quite do that. We'll mail them home on April 12.

It would be great if parents gave us a narrative report—maybe orally?—on the child they see at home. Is that an impossible dream?

—DEBORAH MEIER, *April 2, 2001*

## TEN CLAIMS ABOUT GOOD SCHOOLS

*Every once in a while we all need to make a list, a sort of mantra to reassure ourselves. This letter was such an effort. These lists also serve to sum up ways in which we might differ from other schools, or from the beliefs of even some of our own families. Since complete agreement—even if we could manage to explain our viewpoint clearly enough to be sure one agreed or disagreed with it—is not possible, what then? We assume that disagreements, even with this list of fundamentals—and surely partial disagreements—are healthy for the school and quite tolerable for kids. A little tension between the values and beliefs of school and family are even a good thing.*

Dear Families, Students, Staff, and Friends,

We believe that Mission Hill's five habits of mind, plus strong work habits, are at the heart of being well educated. But success in the real world—what we all want for our children—takes even more.

Here is my top ten list of claims—or propositions—about how to help kids be both well educated and successful. The first six are about what kids need; the last four are about how we teach.

1. All kids need basic skills in literacy and numeracy (the ones we listed in the sheet that went home with students' winter reports).

2. They need to be able to use what they already know to catch on to what they don't yet know. Knowing how to get at what lies underneath surface facts and information is at the core of being well educated. That's what those five habits of mind are about. (They are listed elsewhere.)

3. Kids need social skills. Knowing how to work with others, be a team member, negotiate differences, and stick up for your ideas skillfully is critical to success in the modern world.

4. They need to know how and when to take initiative, not give up easily, and meet deadlines. Perseverance and trustworthiness are, after all the big talk, what colleges, employers, and one's friends are looking for.

5. Having strong personal interests that drive learning is the major distinguishing feature of people who live highly satisfying and significant lives.

6. Kids who have strong connections with interesting adults outside the family are much more likely to succeed.

7. We want kids to be able to handle the real world; therefore, we should be studying the real world—at least some of the time.

8. Human beings learn best when they are interested and engaged; therefore, we shouldn't purposely study things that are boring.

9. No two human beings learn in the same way or at the same speed or age; therefore, we shouldn't try to teach everyone the same way at the same speed or age.

10. Competition and shame don't usually improve learning; therefore, they aren't useful school tools.

We believe the research evidence is overwhelming on each of these ten claims. They tell us a lot about how best to organize a school, what to study, and how. Each has played a role in how we have organized Mission Hill and why we think teaching to standardized tests is cheating kids of a good education and success in the real world.

—DEBORAH MEIER, *February 12, 2001*

## TEACHING TO THE MISSION HILL TEST

*Testing is an ongoing issue for us. We struggle with how to use assessment tools so that they will both motivate and support good student work as well as provide information to student, teacher, family, and world! One tool won't do. It takes a lot of different eyes using lots of different formats; we also need opportunities to compare notes. The student needs to be one of those sets of eyes, and he or she needs to be in the center of the conversation about the data collected. Our final exam—the presentations and defenses of a collection of work in six different domains—tries to exemplify what is going on throughout the years that precede it. It's a more formal and ritualized exercise that calls upon skills, habits, and accomplishments that have been building over the years. In that sense, we are always teaching to "our test." In a state and nation obsessed with standardized tests and where scores on these are the be all and end all, we spend a lot of time explaining our alternative to the MCAS, an alternative we believe matches more closely the real tests of life.*

Dear Families, Students, Staff, and Friends,

"Teaching to the test" doesn't sound like good practice. But it depends on what the test is. In a way, we teach to the test at Mission Hill School all the time—to our test, that is.

The final Big Test at Mission Hill consists of the graduation portfolio exercises that our seventh- and eighth-graders must pass. Practice for these exercises is more focused and intense in the last two years of school here, but it actually starts in kindergarten. All of our studies are aimed at helping kids do well on this kind of exam before they move on to high school.

Our test requires students to demonstrate both knowledge and know-how. We believe that *what* kids learn is important. But it is also important that what we choose to teach helps young people practice the skills they need to pass that final test.

The skills they need are those rigorous intellectual learning habits that Mission Hill is built on: our five essential habits of mind. They also need skills of presentation—both written and oral—that enable people to be persuasive to the larger world. And they need organizational skills—how to organize their time and materials. When the time comes for final exams, they will have to display all of these: subject matter knowledge, thinking habits, communication skills, and organizational skills.

These are worth "teaching to" every day of the week—at home and at school, in the classroom and on the playground.

Now that we've got the final exam set, we hope to create for the ends of third and fifth grades clear "benchmark exams" that mirror the final exam.

The trick is to find ways to help our students use their

minds well—not only in thinking about the material being taught, but also in thinking about what we *don't* teach. In the real world we never confront a problem in exactly the same way twice. It's knowing how to bring our knowledge and skill to bear on novel situations that counts.

There's also "teaching to the test" in the narrower sense. And then, there's teaching to bad tests.

When you take a driver's test, for instance, it's a good idea to know what it is you're going to be tested on. Even if you are an experienced driver, being forewarned helps.

The problem is tougher when the test is not a very good one, covering a lot of things kids don't need to focus on, in formats that are very unreal. Real driving is actually good preparation for the driver's test. Good schooling is not always a good preparation for standardized paper-and-pencil tests.

Fortunately, most of our kids do pretty well on those other tests, like the MCAS and Stanford 9s. It's our own final exam, however, that we're teaching to.

—DEBORAH MEIER, *November 6, 2000*

## A WORLD NOT NEATLY DIVIDED

*Even our short report cards pose challenges to us and our way of seeing children. We try to connect at all times our beliefs and our practices, our views about diversity in the world at large and diversity as it is reflected in our work. Sometimes things are just different, not better or worse. So our short report cards have places to rate, places to check, and lots of places to comment. They are a compromise with time and energy, but we are concerned that parents—and students—feel prepared to disagree, ask for evidence, bring proof that we have got it wrong. Sometimes we have.*

Dear Families, Students, Staff, and Friends,

As we put together our midyear student report cards we always face dilemmas. Report cards require us to make too many not-quite-right choices and to assign too many quick labels.

A recent column in the *New York Times,* with the title "A World Not Neatly Divided," caught my eye for just this reason. It was written by Nobel Laureate economist Amartya Sen, who says that each of us is a mixture of "identities." It's misleading, he argues, to talk about "the Islamic world" or "the Western world," for example. In fact, there are wide diversities and clashes of views in each of these categories.

No nation, religion, culture, or civilization is all of one kind. Each has a long and complicated history. When we fail to remember this, says Sen, we give unwarranted power to some "spokesmen for their 'world,'" thus muffling and silencing others.

Sen concludes that "the robbing of our plural identities not only reduces us; it impoverishes the world." So it is worldwide, and so it is in our little world of Mission Hill, and for each of us as individuals. People don't come neatly packaged or easily summarized.

Our families and staff come from many different racial, ethnic, and language backgrounds. Moreover, we never speak as just parents, just staff, or just a student. We wear different hats, sometimes several at once. And we are often surprised at who takes which position on a particular issue. In short, we are hard to classify.

So, too, with kids, which is why we are so nervous when asked to label them, even as we sometimes must for one reason or another. We try to respectfully describe, leaving room for doubt and uncertainty, knowing that under all labels are individual realities that defy anyone's efforts to sort us neatly. Demystifying labels of all sorts is one of the central tenets of our mission.

So before we say something even as benign as "She's smart," we pause. Then there's "special ed," which can easily become a category of people instead of a label to provide extra support. Even the racial identities we must use to report to funders and other authorities distort the complexity of our staff and student population. So do those check marks on your child's report card.

That's one reason we prefer the narrative reports we do in midwinter; our spring family survey showed parents liked them best too.

Read the report cards we are sending home soon with a grain of salt, then. They are short and to the point, but they can't quite describe your child as a learner. We hope they stimulate our thinking and help us focus our attention. But they are open for discussion. If something in the report seems wrong or misleading when you read it, let us know!

—DEBORAH MEIER, *December 17, 2001*

## THINKING AGAIN ABOUT TESTS

*Our school-site Board of Governors—five parents, five staff, five external members, and two students—play a big role in many important decisions. The most innovative policy they developed (after considerable back and forth) was putting in the hands of each family the decision whether their child would take standardized tests. Instead of trying to come to a single position, and with due regard to the legalities of our relationship to the city and state, we crafted our own approach. We made our views as a staff known, but we agreed to abide by board policy, as long as our larger educational approach was not compromised. It's not always easy to carry this policy out; but we're into the fourth year of the policy and it survives—until we find a better one!*

Dear Families, Students, Staff, and Friends,

It's time once again to think about standardized testing and how best to handle it at Mission Hill School.

Our Governance Board has voted to let parents decide what's best for their own children. We administer the tests—the MCAS in all subjects, and the Stanford 9 as well in those years when there is no math or English language MCAS.

Last year more than 85 percent of the parents of students in grades 2 to 8 asked us not to give the MCAS tests to their children. A smaller number also opted out of the Stanford 9. That was the highest percentage of non-test-takers since we began. The kids who do take the tests get pretty good scores, although it is hard to compare scores from year to year, given our policy.

We try to give families many other ways to know how their children are doing, what they need to work harder on, and where there are problems we need to solve together. The staff unanimously believe that neither the MCAS nor the Stanford 9 helps them to be better teachers. They also think the tests are being misused by the city and state in ways that harm individual children and undermine the educational standards we believe in. They narrow rather than deepen and expand what children study and learn. And they mislabel kids.

The current test mania has brought to new heights a long American love affair with standardized testing. It has never been good for our schools, and it is doing more and more harm. It raises the level of interference by people far from local communities in educational decisions affecting individual children and schools. It is not good for the democratic fabric of the nation.

We do believe in standards—and we believe that children can accomplish far more serious, thoughtful, and rigorous work than has generally been expected of them. All children—not just some so-called gifted and talented ones. We even believe in high-stakes tests, which is what our graduation portfolio review system is all about. But we think such standards should be set by families and school faculty in open and public ways, and that the standards should represent authentic performances of important knowledge and skill. Our curriculum is built on such goals, not on coaching for standardized tests.

In the coming months we'll be sharing information about both standardized tests and alternative forms of assessment. We will let you look at the tests Boston and Massachusetts give, as well as the ones we prefer. Our school policy on testing will be on the agenda of our March board meeting, as well as other house and classroom gatherings.

Remember: the final decisions are in your hands. We will not focus our work on test prep, but we will offer prep sessions to children in grades 4–8 on a limited basis.

—DEBORAH MEIER, *January 14, 2002*

## REAL SCIENCE—AND BOGUS TEST QUESTIONS

*Even our own families sometimes assumed that our opposition to testing was based on a view that academic achievement is not the sole aim of a good school. True enough. But in fact, in our view standardized tests miss the mark in reading and math, and even more so when it comes to achievement in science, history, and other academic disciplines. Schoolwide we studied only one major historical and scientific theme a year, revisited the topics every four years to ensure still greater depth, and required a serious external review of a body of work in each discipline before awarding a diploma. Thus, as we approached the annual spring frenzy, we tried to make clearer the distinction between our tests and the state's tests. Providing actual examples was one of our favorite techniques; families could then actually see and try out the differences.*

Dear Families, Students, Staff, and Friends,

Last year's MCAS science test raises troubling questions about what it really measures. Many of the frameworks, or broad definitions, that the test is based on are sensible enough. But in translating them into test items something has gone very wrong. Here's an example. One of the state standards for learning science is that "students engage in problem solving, establishing evidence, searching for connections, and the process of inquiry." Who would quarrel with this? Surely not us. In fact, it sounds like this standard was cribbed from the Mission Hill Habits of Mind.

But here's one of the test items that's supposed to tell us whether students meet this standard:

> The suspension system of a truck includes the
> A. engine and carburetor
> B. wheels and axles
> C. brakes and muffler
> D. steering wheel and speedometer

Knowing the right answer (it's B) has little if anything to do with solving problems or searching for connections. This and many other MCAS test items ask students only to identify isolated facts, removed from any context of scientific inquiry. Teaching to this test will not lead to good science learning.

Our school habits of mind are at the heart of real science, and of our work this winter. But they can be learned only by using them—over and over—in real scientific investigations.

Last week in Geralyn's room a group of kids was trying to create chain reactions with dominoes. I watched, and then (to paraphrase science writer Chet Raymo) for a moment time stood still for me. I got totally absorbed in trying to create a chain reaction that just wouldn't work: to get the dominoes to fall in a right-angle turn. I gave up. But Menelik, Sophie, and Matteo took it on and produced, on their own initiative, a set of experiments that came close to achieving our goal. They understood the need to develop a reproducible experimental design. It was genuine science; we were all amazed at what we found out. A group of block and ramp builders—McKenzie, William, Kieran, and Grace—worked on a similar challenge. They grabbed me later in the hall and made me come in to see what they had accomplished.

A video clip of kids in Emily's class engaged in scientific explorations on electricity was equally exciting. In fact, as I go from room to room, I see students deeply engaged in scientific challenges, and sticking to them in ways that suggest we're definitely on the right road—respecting both the poetic side and the tough, careful, investigative side of science. Real science respects trial and error, wonder, and creativity—not the memorizing of irrelevant facts for a bureaucratic test.

—DEBORAH MEIER, *January 7, 2000*

## FOUR ARGUMENTS AGAINST THE TESTS

*There are more than four good arguments, but these seem to us to be the most important. It's necessary, however, to repeat this discussion from time to time because standardized testing rep-*

*resents a big and tough decision for many families. The dilemma, as the Governance Board was aware, is how to be fair to parents who in fact want their kids to take such tests. There are a variety of reasons why parents might wish to do so: They may be considering a school that counts the test score; or they may think that the test is a way to prepare for "later on." Other times they may want to "check out" whether our claims about their kids are accurate; and at still other times, they decide on the test because a child wants to take it. We try to make all the kids feel good about their family's decision, but we've probably not prepared the test takers as well as they could be prepared. How to have our cake and eat it too remains a puzzle.*

Dear Families, Students, Staff, and Friends,

Two weeks ago, I wrote that the current test mania in the U.S. is doing more and more harm. I want to be very clear about the reasons I feel so strongly about standardized testing.

1. Standardized tests are being used improperly, in ways that were never intended. They were designed to measure "I.Q." or "aptitude"—something fixed, to be measured once or twice in a lifetime. That idea itself is suspect. But as James Popham, a leading test expert, says, mere cosmetic changes such as calling them "achievement" tests don't change what they're able to do. Robert Linn, another leader in testing, reminds us that, above all, the tests were never designed to be "taught to."

2. The measurement error is enormous. The same test given to the same student on a different day can yield a wildly different score. Averaged over a large population,

these errors tend to balance each other out. But the tests are invalid at the individual score level.

3. The multiple-choice, right/wrong format can't capture achievement. Neither can mini-essays scored by people who must read them in a minute or less. These features of standardized tests make them fast and cheap to administer and score, but they compound their inaccuracy.

4. Standardized tests exclude most of what, in the real world (including college), defines being well educated.

It's as if we decided that the written portion of the driver's test was all that mattered, and we spent all our energy in driver's ed raising kids' scores on that part. Then, to make sure no one thought we were going soft, we made the questions really hard (how does fuel injection affect performance of catalytic converters?) and added open-ended writing tasks (describe what to do when your left rear tire blows out while driving at 55 miles per hour). Then, just to show you were raising standards, you counted spelling and punctuation. Fine. But such a test wouldn't actually distinguish a good from a bad driver. Ditto for these tests. They miss everything that matters: reading with a critical mind, not getting fooled by nonsense, and knowing how to persuade, work well with others, take leadership, stick to a task, meet deadlines, be reliable in a crunch, or take initiative.

The tests are good for one thing: ranking people (and schools and districts). And they have always done a good job of making sure the winners in the rest of life's stakes stay ahead and the losers stay behind. That's not by accident. (More on that later.)

So Mission Hill is sticking with tests of actual performance—the things that really count. We'll teach kids some of the tricks of testing, partly because they're interesting and partly because if kids take tests they should know a bit about how they work.

—DEBORAH MEIER, *January 28, 2002*

## GRADUATION BY PERFORMANCE

*This was written on the eve of our first graduation, which was a squeaker. One or two kids just made it by the deadline. The kids were the first to try our school out, and not all the decisions we made along the way turned out to be quite right (and some were changed for future graduates). It was the first time I had watched the process for kids of this age. But the way the kids took to it, the quality of the work they performed, and the responses we got from outside reviewers and family members made us solid converts to this approach.*

Dear Families, Students, Staff, and Friends,

Watching my advisee, Akwasi, in his final portfolio presentations in math and art the other day reminded me of how wonderful our Mission Hill graduation-by-performance standards are.

Akwasi taught his graduation committee how to scale back a recipe, described how he revised his graphs to ensure that he had comparable data, explained why you need common denominators, discussed why he prefers Jackson Pollack to Salvador Dalí, and shared with us his newfound pleasure in art. What a pleasure it was, also, to watch a video of a play he wrote, acted in, and co-directed.

Each of our twelve eighth-graders is going through a similar process. We come together as a staff at lunch and at the end of the day boasting and telling anecdotes about our advisees. Some of them have had to go back for a second or third try. And one or two may even need extra time before we sign off.

But it's always rewarding to see their progress. It reaffirms our work as a school and the process of assessment we have designed.

Sometimes it gives us reason to pause and consider ways to improve our work so that the kids' performances are stronger. This should not be a time for last-minute cramming for exams but a chance to show off real mastery. Yet some kids are still cramming. We don't always get this right. But these eighth-graders—our pilot crew—give strong evidence that we're going the right way. They have led the way. Thanks to every one of you: Akwasi, Ian, Rebeca, Vaper, Ariel, Jeffrey, Chris, Janina, Davide, Victor, Nefta, and Latalia.

Heidi Lyne has produced, with help from the Carnegie Foundation, a twenty-five-minute video to illustrate the portfolio process (warts and all) and its rationale. It has helped us think about how to prepare kids for these kinds of exams. We hope to update it regularly and to show it to kids and families many times over the coming years.

The immense amount of self-assessment that our kids and teachers do has provided the critical feedback so important to becoming an educated person. Some people used to speak of our kind of schooling as "learning by doing." Actually, it's learning by thinking, doing, reflecting, and then redoing. Over and over. If something is worth learning, your attitude can't be "been there, done that." Even final examinations at Mission Hill are about work in progress. Over the years, each of these students will revisit the work they did here many times, get better and better, go deeper and deeper.

We hope that our students' parents and families are having almost as much fun watching the kids learn as we are. Maybe you're even learning something alongside them—just as we are.

—DEBORAH MEIER, *May 29, 2001*

# The Letters on Standards from Parker

## GETTING GRADES

*One of Parker's guiding principles is that internal motivation is ultimately more lasting and rewarding than external motivation. To students, this often translates into the fact that we "don't give grades." In time, most of them realize that, in fact, we do assess their work, not only very carefully but also with important consequences, such as how swiftly they are able to master various skills in order to be promoted through our curriculum divisions and eventually to graduate. Each piece of work is judged as "Just Beginning," "Approaching," "Meeting," or "Exceeding" their teachers' expectations for good work in the next, more demanding arena. A paper earning a Just Beginning would not "count" (that is, would not be included in a gateway or graduation portfolio) unless it was improved.*

*These "grades" are fluid rather than static, but no matter how flexible and helpful we are determined to be, we are also serious about the challenges that we expect our students to be able to meet and overcome.*

Dear Families,

A student who left Parker last June to go to another high school dropped in recently on some of her former teachers who were gathered to define their expectations for this year's students. "I miss you," she started off, and was assured that she was missed as well. Then she overcame her shyness and blurted out what had clearly been on her mind. "I'm not sure I will ever again have as good teachers as there are at Parker. But I need to get grades. I can already see that it's doing me some good."

Grades. Expectations. Motivation. Improvement. What do these large and important concepts have to do with one another? How can they be woven together to produce the best possible result for every child? Every school struggles with it.

The reason Parker doesn't "give grades," I believe, is that grades emphasize a rather unimportant part of assessment: the competitive part. Grades tell a student where she or he ranked in a certain class on a specific assignment. One got an "A" because one did as well as could be expected of that particular group of people. Given another group of people—or another kind of assignment—one's grade might well have been different. A teacher in a school where I used to work handed papers back in order: from the best job done on this particular test to the worst. When we chastised him about it, he defended the practice by saying that every time he handed papers back, the line-up was different. All a student had to do to rank more highly was to work harder. It was a series of snapshots: no more, no less. Or so he claimed.

When Parker teachers assess their students' work, they try to avoid group photos. Instead, they train their video camera on one student to focus on the quality of his or her journey. They notice the student's habits: Do details support generalizations? Is the writing interesting to read? Are real points being made? Are sentences laid out carefully enough and words spelled correctly enough to be considered genuine communication? How does this piece of work compare to his last one? What would be the appropriate piece of work for her to try next?

In deemphasizing competition—"group snapshots"—we are recognizing the vagaries of groupings. We are trying to reduce the hubris at one end of the scale and the discouragement at the other, both of which can lead a kid to stop trying. We are preparing our students for a world in which their ability to assess their own progress and to work with others will largely determine their long-range success.

One thing is for sure: we all need to know what others think of our work. "Bad" reports are a reality check. "Good" ones make us feel appreciated, and that's an important part of motivation. I remember a student who passed the "B" barrier years ago, somewhat miraculously—we both agreed on that—and then never fell below it again. Why? Was it greater maturity on her part? Or the bad habits of the group she was being compared with? Was it my elaborate explanation of exactly what she had done well? Or was it "bragging rights," which became too sweet to give up?

As for ranking, it makes us feel wonderful when our ex-student tells us that as teachers we are the "best." That's an "A" in anyone's book, and we are proud to have achieved it. Still, at Parker, "A" stands for "Approaching," and we need to improve. We need to help our students to consider our form of assessment to be as meaningful and as motivating as any other. And more than any other group, I believe, it's their parents who will be able to help us with that part of our collective job.

—NANCY SIZER, *October 2, 1998*

## ANSWERING TOUGH QUESTIONS

*Parker practices promotion by performance. In order to move from Division I and its junior high curriculum into Division II and its beginning high school work, a student must have a substantial portfolio and a persuasive cover letter that demonstrates that he or she is ready to tackle more advanced assignments in a number of areas. Once the teachers agree, a gateway is organized with his family, a few chosen friends, teachers, and other visitors. The young man in this example was demonstrating his readiness in the Arts and Humanities area. Two confessions: In my twenty-five years in my own classroom, I was the ultimate mother hen, protecting my chicks from all manner of ignorance and possible unfairness. For most of those years, the idea of a stranger's standing in a gateway and helping to decide whether a student was ready to be promoted was not only unfamiliar; it was heresy. Yet I also knew that if what I was trying to teach them was really to be valuable to them, it would also have to be valid and impressive to more than just one teacher. Hence the "jury" the idea that an idea, a piece of work, or even a careful answer to a question, can be judged in an open forum by objective others, even when the students are relatively young. The other confession, of course, is that I was the "guest" who asked the temporarily nasty question.*

Dear Families,

"You claim that this judge in *A Civil Action* was unfair," a guest commented to a student in his gateway into Division II. "What makes you say that?"

Students at Parker are told from the beginning that they will be expected to present their work in public and that they will need to answer questions about it. Some questions will be familiar ones, coming out of the classes that preceded the piece of work. Other questions, however, may reflect the experience or perspective of the questioner and thus be somewhat unpredictable.

Our word for this process is "jurying," by which we mean that we and our students subject ourselves to the analysis and judgment of strangers. Gently at first, but increasing in seriousness and unpredictability as the students grow older, we ask them to explain and defend their work. Although the atmosphere is supportive and collegial, we expect them to answer tough questions, and then more questions.

The circumstances vary. A parent who is a scientist may travel around the exhibits on space during demonstration night and may discuss a project with the student who designed and presented it. A visitor may be asked to provide formal feedback, which is shared with the student and the student's teacher. Although most of this feedback is in the form of suggestions rather than outright criticism, the process can be an instructive one.

In each succeeding gateway, the students can expect more probing questions, ones that may seem to put them on the spot. They need to develop the preparation and presence of mind to perform well under those circumstances. And already in our young history, some students are presenting their work to college admissions officers who are evaluating not only the student but also our school by the quality of their presentations and their answers to the visitors' sometimes quite pointed questions. Recently, an admissions officer said, "You know, there are a lot of alternative schools these days, and some of them are pretty flaky. But I can see from the way you are all speaking that Parker is serious about its students' work." This was an important juried Exhibition. It seems that now—and for that admissions officer—Parker passed the test. Whew!

Our aim for Parker graduates is that a stranger will find them to be knowledgeable and enthusiastic about something that they are learning at school. But for now, we'll return to our thirteen-year-old's gateway. After a moment, the student looked over briefly to his teacher. She was calm, confident of his ability to deal with the question. She reminded him to refer to his text, a book that he had read very well. Of course! He remembered a series of details, which in only a few well-crafted sentences, did much to incriminate the judge. It was a superb answer, one that would have satisfied the sternest and most objective jury. As with so many gateways, there was an air of triumph in the room. He was put on the spot; he had to rely on his own memory, his own logic, his own powers of persuasion, and he came through. He is well on his way into a life that will be spent answering questions with confidence and effectiveness.

—NANCY SIZER, *October 16, 1998*

## MCAS

*State standardized testing arrived during our watch at Parker. On scholarly grounds, many of us had little confidence in the approach. Many—with justification, it turned out—feared its abuse. Nonetheless, principals of public schools are officers of the state. I felt the need to speak in that role, albeit with the reservations I felt. This was a difficult letter to write.*

Dear Families,

In a few weeks we will receive Parker students' scores on the Massachusetts Comprehensive Assessment System (MCAS) tests. Whatever the results for each of

Parker's students, we should all be both respectful of and skeptical about this extraordinarily onerous assessment.

Tests tell us something. They give us all a sense of how each child does on this sort of exercise. They provide teachers with information parallel to theirs but gathered in a different way. With the tingle of competition, they focus student, teacher, and parent attention on learning. They reflect what state authorities believe is important, and in so doing shape the curriculum. Cross-school comparisons can be useful. Massachusetts testing is serious business.

At the same time, we all must recognize that a timed, standardized test can tell us only some things about a student: Whether the school taught those aspects of a subject that were presented on the test (and, if so, whether he really has his head around them). Whether he can connect what he knows to what is presented to him in what might be a new way. Whether he is cool and persistent under pressure.

Such a test cannot tell us much about other things. Whether a student is brilliant in a discipline though relatively unfamiliar with what happened to be tested. Whether she thinks deeply, but slowly. Whether she has absorbing interests and shows grit in pursuing them. Whether she is highly imaginative (indeed, many tests discriminate against the imaginative, given the standardized manner in which even "open-ended" questions are assigned points). Whether she can think on her feet, speak well and clearly, and bring understandings from one subject to the illumination of another. Whether she is thoughtful as a matter of habit.

Let's give the scores soon to arrive our careful respect. Let us use them to help our school. Let's also keep them in perspective. Tests are like taking a patient's temperature in the hospital; they tell us something important but hardly all that is important. State scores should be part of our picture of each student's work, something to be judiciously considered, taken neither as all illuminating nor without merit. They are a serious part of our business in public education.

—TED SIZER, *October 23, 1998*

## STUDENTS "SELLING" PARKER

*One of my jobs during the 1998–1999 school year was to function as a transition counselor. This job had two parts. First, I was essentially an assistant to the parents' Life After Parker Committee; second, I worked with students intending to graduate in 2000 regarding goals and good options. These titles had been chosen, I assumed, with the idea that any respectable short-term future was to be both enabled and applauded in our school; but of course in most minds, the idea of college was paramount. I had two special challenges: The first was to keep all our minds open about the variety of post-secondary placements that might be good places for our graduates. (By so doing, I hoped to avoid having big crowds before some of the booths and no one in front of others at the college fairs I had been asked to advertise.) The second big challenge was to con-*

*vince many of our students that there would actually* be *a "life after Parker." They were pretty good at setting goals within the Parker setting, but since they were the oldest students in the school, they had no predecessors from whom to learn about the experience of getting into college.*

Dear Families,

A couple of weeks ago I spoke with a young friend who is helping five small new progressive public schools with college admissions. They are essentially doing the same work that we are doing here at Parker: "selling" their schools now in order to be able to "sell" their students in years to come. She and her colleagues in the schools are making connections, deciding how to present themselves, and learning as much as they can about the colleges that might appeal to their students. This is important institutional work, and it is crucial that we do it well. It is why the Life After Parker Task Force has been working so hard for a number of years.

My friend was optimistic. She said that many colleges had told her that they were looking for exactly the kinds of students we are trying to create. "They want students who know what they are interested in, who know how to see a project through, who are not afraid of answering questions, who can benefit from criticism, who are willing to take charge of their own learning," she said. "They have told me that they are tired of getting blobby kids who just want to sit there and let life happen to them. The colleges are complaining that they actually have to 'un-teach' some of those students! They want kids who are ready to plunge in on the first day of college. They have found this to be true of other Coalition kids, so they are willing to take a chance on us."

There was a workshop on college admissions and even a college booth at the fall forum, so I tried out my friend's theory on the college's dean of admissions and dean of students. They had just come from a panel given by a school not too different from ours in which students presented some pieces of their work. The dean of students, who had worked in several colleges, said that she was the one who had led the standing ovation at the end of the panel. She declared that my friend is right to be confident, no matter how new a school may be, "as long as your kids can do what those kids did."

We may need to "sell" our school, but we are convinced that our students are our best salespeople. Twice already—last year and earlier this fall—our own Parker student presenters have earned the equivalent of a standing ovation when we have gathered college people here at Parker. Next Thursday afternoon, November 19, a few of them will again present their work to the colleges that attend our college forum. (For more information about each of the colleges, see elsewhere in these announcements). We need to keep that meeting relatively small, so only the Life after Parker parents and a few teachers will come to that part of the forum. Between 6:00 and 7:00, however, we hope that a large number of Parker students, parents, and teachers will come to the lower vault to meet the admissions officers, pick up their wares, practice question-asking skills, and engage in some very interesting conversation. We want the colleges to learn about us, but at this point in our history it is becoming equally important to learn about them, so we can be wise consumers as well as effective salesmen.

—NANCY SIZER, *November 13, 1998*

## GATEWAY: A NEW VERB

*Twice a year Parker arranges for gateways, a public review of a student's portfolio and an oral Exhibition about his or work—as demonstration that the student is ready to enter the next and higher division. Especially for the younger students, faculty members counsel families to let their student gateway only when the evidence is clear that success is highly likely. Parents needed to understand why Parker functions in this way—and to be reminded and reassured that the school was determined that every student legitimately met the standard, however long it took.*

Dear Families,

**gate way** ('gāt-wā) v. 1. To present one's schoolwork to an audience of outsiders (spec: Parker School) 2. To get a step up in life.

This is gateway time. Mid-January this year finds Parker students who feel ready to move up to the next division exhibiting for all of us—and for themselves—the work they have completed. That is, they "go public," explaining not only what they have mastered but how they have mastered it.

At the start, Parker called these public sessions gateways. In a flash a new verb was invented. "I am gatewaying this Thursday." "Let's gateway Ruth and Eric this June." The new usage is now deep in the school's common language.

A gateway takes time for students, their teachers, and their parents. We justify this on educational grounds. First, preparing a portfolio of one's best work from over a couple of years is a superb form of revision. What was it that I learned? Did I express that learning clearly? Do I know what I need to know well enough to answer questions about it? Can I use ideas and facts that I studied perhaps eighteen months ago?

Second, the process of collecting and defending one's work forces a student to reflect on her own learning against a demanding common standard. Whatever our ages, we are all more effective if we know how and why and when we learn. The earlier one gets that knowledge, the better each of us will perform.

Third, a teacher cannot know well whether a student fully understands something without discussion. He may display something to us—an "answer," the result usually of memorization and much more. Unless we probe the reasons for that answer, thereby getting to what lies underneath his thinking, we cannot know whether that young person has a truly deep—and thus sustainable—grasp of an idea, approach, or skill.

Finally, a gateway is an opportunity for a student to

show off, to demonstrate for teachers, parents, friends, and visitors what she can do with her knowledge. Publicly displayed success is an elixir, deservedly so for people of all ages. Look at me. Listen to me. See what I can do. From such feeling of authentic mastery comes the courage to push ahead to a higher level, for a Parker student whether that is Division II, Division III, or college.

Gatewaying, under other names, has a long history. The seventeenth-century colonial colleges gave degrees on the basis of public Recitations and Disputations. The nineteenth-century academies called these exercises Exhibitions. Throughout, the emphasis was on a person's own progress rather than comparisons of individuals and institutions that so dominate talk of standards in our own era. Parker is happy to give new life—and a new verb—to this ancient, demanding, and respectful process.

—TED SIZER, *January 22, 1998*

## FINE COMPARED WITH WHAT?

*When the MCAS scores arrived, everyone—students, parents, teachers—were nervous, and many annoyed, even infuriated. All of us, even the youngest, however, were familiar with testing. How did you know what you knew if not confirmed in some reliable way? What an externally derived score meant was another matter. Parents needed to be reassured that much of growing up is wonderfully mysterious and that making too much of any one score at any one time was unwise and ultimately unnecessary. (I picked the name Hobart as no student had the name or another close to it.)*

Dear Families,

"How's my son Hobart doing?" you ask. "Fine, just fine. Nice boy," I answer. We smile, nod at one another. If Hobie had been present, he would cringe. The question, of course, is too vague and the answer a bit of evasive treacle.

If I had guts and knew you well, I would ask, "Fine compared with what?" Fine against some absolute standard such as a PSAT or MCAS score? Fine compared with what Hobie appeared to be like two months ago? Fine compared with my personal judgment of his capabilities? Fine compared with the perceived standards of other schools, that is fine against how he might be doing at Acton Boxborough? Fine against my personal hunch about where a kid of Hobie's age should be in this frustratingly vague process of growing up? The judgments of "fine"-ness might be radically different in each case.

If I were feeling expansive as well as frank, I might ask, "Fine in his schoolwork or fine in life?" You might wonder, indeed even query, by what conceit I would concern myself about Hobie's overall life. I would reply that fine-ness in school is conditioned by fine-ness in life. A kid distracted at home might do more poorly in Building 2602 than one at peace at the kitchen table. On the other hand, Hobie might be an adroit compartmentalizer, with home and school in disassociated boxes. A zombie at home, a genius at school, or vice versa.

The ultimate frankness between us would be to consider how Hobie was doing against all of these "compared with what" options. Against one standard he might be fine, against another unimpressive, against a third wonderfully remarkable. None of us of any age is reducible to an arbitrary, single index, "fine" on some test, fine on one essay, fine on a bit of help to the community. Thank goodness we are all more interesting than that.

And in the end, what you and I ultimately agreed upon would be ephemeral. Hobie will be different a month from now. "What in heaven's name happened to Hobie?" might be your question to me a month hence. "I haven't a clue," I might answer. "Let's just blame it on growing up."

—TED SIZER, *March 12, 1999*

# Acknowledgments

All the constituents that make up the Mission Hill Community, too many to name individually, truly made this book possible. These letters were written as part of an on-going dialogue between parents, students, and staff—plus an occasional other reader out there somewhere in the world. Those readers include even the superintendent of Boston's public schools, Tom Payzant, whose support for pilot schools in Boston made Mission Hill possible in the first place, and whose timely responses to key issues raised in the newsletter over the years helped us solve one dilemma after another. Thanks in particular go to Brian Straughter, my amazing co-principal, who now writes every other letter, and to those staff members who are also joining in.

I've been writing letters home, first as a classroom teacher and then as a principal, week in and week out for nearly forty years. When (and if) I finally do really retire, I'll miss it a lot. Especially since I've had such great help putting the newsletters together. Help came first from Ed Miller, who for six years edited my Mission Hill columns so they'd fit in the prescribed space and nudged everyone else until he had a whole issue every week. He also nudged me to think about what I meant to say, an important editorial habit of mind. Dani Coleman has taken over this task, and Helen Fouhey and Brian are always there as backups. I'm enormously indebted to them for their advice—on both technical matters and content. Since I often circulate drafts beforehand, I'm also influenced by the sharp but kind notes from various colleagues, sometimes in disagreement, other times adding a point or correcting a mistake. Thank you all. And thank you to Happie Byers, who has been collecting my columns for decades upon decades for just this reason!

Working with Andy Hrycyna at Beacon for the third time has been a pleasure. His ear for what it is I'm trying to say has always been indispensable—not only, I hope, in improving the writing but also the ideas. Thanks again, Andy, as well as others at Beacon who have moved this book along.

And then there are Nancy and Ted, whom I discovered

when I was fifty. They have been important allies and, above all, important friends; they have made my life interesting in ways I never anticipated.

DEBORAH MEIER

We owe much to the trustees of the Francis W. Parker Charter Essential School for permitting us to publish these letters to the school's families—and even more for allowing us to serve as the acting co-principals during the 1998–1999 academic year. For us it was an extraordinary and happy thirteen months.

We are grateful to the families to whom we wrote these letters. Their patience and support of us was generous; they made us feel as if we were indeed part of a worthy dialogue. We also have a debt to Carin Algava and Bridget Towle, who supported our writing and were patient with us when it arrived at the eleventh hour before mailing.

As always, the staff at Beacon Press, and especially our enthusiastic and imaginative editor, Andy Hrycyna, have been a joy to work with.

We are honored to share this volume with Deborah Meier and the community at Mission Hill School in Boston. Deborah has been and remains a close friend, a soul sister on matters of schooling and democracy, and a model of teacher/scholar for us all.

TED AND NANCY SIZER